NIETZSCHE

UNPUBLISHED LETTERS

NIETZSCHE
UNPUBLISHED LETTERS

Translated and edited by

KURT F. LEIDECKER

PHILOSOPHICAL LIBRARY

New York

Printed in the United States of America

ISBN: 978-0-8022-1220-7

INTRODUCTION

Because the beauty of the overman came to him as a shadow Nietzsche asked no longer for the gods. Instead he felt creatively impelled toward man. This he confesses in *Ecce Homo*. Creation, now, is definitely man's concern. Whoever creates must also be harsh; he cannot show pity toward whatever feels the keen edge of the chisel. And Nietzsche did put the chisel and hammer to human flesh and spirit in his books, *Thus Spoke Zarathustra, Beyond Good and Evil, The Twilight of the Idols, Ecce Homo,* and the others.

While thus in his volumes he addressed himself to man in general, in his letters he spoke to individuals, living persons known to him. And how different do these letters strike us from the books even on first reading. It is as if Zarathustra had become human, nearly all-too-human. In the letters Nietzsche is the typical university student, the devoted son, the shy and distant lover, the sensitive friend. So fragile is the delicacy of his tenderly reared friendships that he handles them like the choicest of Meissen China, never inelegantly in the manner of idol-smashers.

The Nietzsche of the letters is the man who abandoned the ruggedness of his mountain cave to seek, yes, frantically crave, the least stirrings of kindness, who may even be content with decency and plain

1

courtesy. A great and healthy love, free of quasi Oedipus and *anima* complexes, had he experienced it, would have probably placed him in the seventh heaven and his heart and mouth would have uttered mellower and more pleasing prophesies. The Nietzsche of the great books which, to borrow a phrase of Thoreau's, "do not allow themselves to be read" by everybody, had reasons to consider himself a destiny; the Nietzsche of the ever so gentle, quite perfect letters was a walking tragedy. And tragedy, despite its dark, unfathomable and mystic sides is closer to Everyman than is cold, cutting, irrational destiny. Thus, generally speaking, the letters constitute the easy introduction, the psychological guide to a personality which, nevertheless, remains vastly complex, gigantic, aleatory.

But this is only one recommendation for the letters.

Great men,—and not even his enemies will deny greatness of one quality or another in Nietzsche—sow seeds, and their gardens blossom and sprout in later years with other strange plants. And since age confers a special sanctity the words and ways of thinkers of the past are made to justify the actions of the present. The huge historic events between Nietzsche and us today were, of course, the two World Wars and the rise and fall of powerful ideologies. In these again so-called Prussianism, power politics, secularism and anti-Semitism played important roles, and since Nietzsche had to say something on all of these issues he has been brought into the fray.

The antagonists of German politics, be it Kaiser Wilhelm's or Hitler's, blamed Nietzsche, for one, for what they censured and even hated. Had he not preached the Gospel of strength, called himself the anti-Christ, apotheosized the superman? Had not Germany officially shown new interest in Nietzsche and honored his memory? *Ergo,* it must be true that Nietzsche had been the evil genius right along.

Of course, the serious students of Nietzsche's works were always few, and fewer yet were those who discovered sense in his writings. Then there were those who studied the man as one would peruse an interesting school example of luetic paranoia, megalomania, weird complexes and drives. What they wrote in consequence made to some mentalities more entertaining reading than Nietzsche's own aphorisms. Yet, the trouble was that none understood the whole man, deducing quite often a pseudoknowledge from particular aspects of his life and thought. Hence, all were right, or wrong, up to a point.

It was August 7, 1937, that Dr. Wilhelm Hoppe and Professor Karl Schlechta announced to the Committee of the Critical Historical Complete Edition of the Works and Letters of Nietzsche, in Hitler's Germany, mind you, their sensational findings regarding the falsifications of Nietzsche's letters and unpublished material by his sister Elisabeth Förster-Nietzsche. Since then new interest has sprung up around the greatly stereotyped picture of the man, and new evaluations are called for, confusing and, no doubt, confounding an already perplexing topic.

The result has been, on the whole, favorable to the portrait of Nietzsche in the eyes of those whose ideologies were triumphant in the recent armed conflict, while those who lost the war see themselves somewhat duped. All in all, a truer Nietzsche has emerged, a kindlier, more tolerant man, a man who had, and lived, a single heterodox purpose practically from his student days, whose loneliness and desertion

3

by nearly everyone drove him to accentuate his thesis more brusquely as the years went by and flagrantly so when paresis of the brain removed the inhibitions his stoical nature had so valiantly upheld.

A whole catalogue of evils, thirsts and shocking utterances with which Nietzsche has been charged needs now a more sympathetic reconsideration, especially in view of the existentialist legitimate philosophical claims as well as popular infatuations, and the letters make it easier. Our judgments, henceforth, should be made less flippantly. The contradictions, particularly, with which Nietzsche has been so glibly charged, should be re-examined. They include the persons and events around Nietzsche. Just in passing let us mention a few.

Nietzsche loved the German language and considered himself a great master of it, greater than even Luther and Goethe; yet he extolled other languages and literatures. He had hard words to say about the Jews, yet he denounced anti-Semitism in clear terms. He loved and revered Richard Wagner as a father and genius; yet he nastily broke with him. He preached strength, force and self-assertion to the point of brutality; yet he reproached himself for having pity as second nature, a weakness for which he blamed reading Schopenhauer and being influenced by him. All the world is persuaded that "superman," "will to power," and "master race" are Nietzsche's dubious gifts appreciated principally, if not wholly, by the Germans alone; yet the Jew Georg Brandes informed him that the Scandinavians understood these concepts even better by virtue of their Icelandic tradition. During his unadumbrated lifetime the German intellectuals showed complete indifference to Nietzsche and were the first ones to brand him immoralist. This treatment drove him to insist on his Polish origin, indeed, that he was a Pole, and not a German at all. Zarathustra was never averse to a good fight, and Nietzsche in his youth was a cavalryman and cannoneer; yet he acquired Swiss citizenship to think and write in peace to recreate the world in thunder and lightning. We shall not touch upon the apparent and/or real contradictions in the philosophical utterances of Nietzsche, the great "yea-sayer" and "nihilist" all in one.

Nietzsche was often plagued by the thought that his work might fall into the hands of persons totally unsuited to expound or edit his writings. It was the irony of fate that one person close to him, his own sister Elisabeth, should become the worst offender, she who could write endearing letters, on occasion kept house for him, took care of him while his mind was enshrouded, collected his writings after his death and established the Nietzsche Archives. That most everyone would misunderstand or not understand him at all, to that Nietzsche had soon become reconciled after publishing his challenging writings; it was the price he had to pay for being a prophet. But he always had apprehensions regarding his sister, and they were fully justified. He knew how selfish she could be, how vituperative, how jealous of his affections, and he sensed the danger. Letters prove it, the nickname he gave her, Llama, prove it, for does not a llama spit chidingly when irked? He knew she did not, could not follow his flight of thought and he forgave her as he did his friends whom he nevertheless respected. But there were other more serious discrepancies of a highly personal, sometimes even religious nature.

Elisabeth's possessiveness slackened when she married Bernhard Förster, an avowed anti-Semite, whom she followed to Paraguay to found a *Nueva Germania* for the purpose of racial purification. When he died she returned to Germany. Time had run out on Nietzsche's light moments. She herself stood in need of income. The brother was now becoming famous. Here was a perfect opportunity in which she even would not let her mother share completely: She would become sole owner and executrix of her brother's estate, including editor of any and all letters he had written. In this way letters not all flattering to her could be manipulated in her favor, so could others addressed to their mother. An erasure or ink-spot in the right place, either in the heading or in the closing would do the trick. Letters could also be fabricated and some of the original drafts which the brother used to make could be turned to advantage, especially when the addressee was not clearly to be ascertained. At all events she had to be cleared of any allegations or suggestions that there were or ever had been any but slight disagreements and quarrels between her and Fritz. That there had been was, of course, known to many friends whom Nietzsche had apprised. That mutual trust and affection ultimately triumphed after every dissonance between brother and sister could be proven once she would have in her possession all letters proving the contrary. These she got by gift or purchase and then proceeded to present an amiable, consistent picture of her relationship to her brother to the reading public.

Nobody, of course, suspected anything until Professor Karl Schlechta noticed in the Nietzsche Archives letters which were singed, torn or had ink-spots in crucial places. Letters to their mother, Franziska Nietzsche, appeared in print as addressed to her.

Other irregularities were discovered. In her ambition, fanned by a swelling wave of nationalism, she played up supporting materials in Nietzsche's life and writings, such as his relation to Wagner in which she de-emphasized his differences with the great composer. Nietzsche's name was, thus, swept into the orbit of Nationalist Socialist ideology, one famous supporter the more, but also one head the more on whom antiracists, anti-Germans, antimilitarists, anti-anti-Semites could heap further blame and contempt.

Of course, the Elisabeth Förster-Nietzsche case is not the only one of its kind. What man, no longer able to speak for himself, has not played a similar role, and what other Elisabeths have not done similarly with or without conscience? Surely, these machinations could have been discovered earlier had not readers of Nietzsche's works been so careless, hurried and superficial.[1] Nietzsche's closest friends, Overbeck and Peter Gast knew of them and expected the worst. But, owing to Professor Schlechta's edition of the works of Nietzsche in three volumes,[2] with the third volume bringing the literary remains as they were before they were edited under supervision of the sister, and the letters with the text-critical apparatus, we can say now that we have a competent edition which will enable anyone to attain a truer, more clarified conception of Nietzsche's life and thinking.

As to the letters translated here, most of them for the first time, they represent a selection from the 278 letters excellently chosen and published by Schlechta in the third volume just referred to. If read chronologically, a good picture may be obtained of the mental and emotional development of Nietzsche. One thing should be apparent to every reader, that almost from the beginning Nietzsche was conscious of an important mission he had to fulfill in life as well as of the gravity and unusual nature of the message he was to bear.

The letters to his sister Elisabeth (Liese, Lisbeth; Llama, etc.) and his mother—his father, a Lutheran clergyman, had died in 1849 when he was but five years of age—show him affectionate, tender, conciliatory in differences, always ready to seek understanding after misunderstandings. The sister was, no doubt, one of the weightiest factors in his life. She could be sweet and helpful. Her jealousy of men and women who drew "Fritzchen's" attention away from her, may even betray more than sisterly love. She was the source of difficulties and scenes, and nearly succeeded in alienating the mother from her son.

Next in importance was Richard Wagner who, some maintain, substituted for his father. Immense admiration for the man never left him despite his disagreements when Wagner had entered his Parsifal stage. As soon as Nietzsche noticed the forebodings of feelings of need for confession, contrition, and absolution in Wagner, he felt quite forlorn. Yet he could not help writing to Peter Gast:[3] "I confess, real terror is overcoming me when I realize again *how* closely I am, indeed, *related* to Wagner."

Cosima Wagner was Nietzsche's womanly ideal. Thinking himself Dionysus he worshipped her as Ariadne. He became intimately acquainted with both Cosima and Richard Wagner when he had accepted a professorship in philology at Basel, Switzerland. These and other biographical data may be gathered from his letter to Georg Brandes of April 10, 1888, translated below as No 60, which may profitably be read first.

8

Two friendships are noteworthy going back to his student days, the lasting one with Paul Deussen who later became the outstanding authority in Indian philosophy, and that with Erwin Rohde, the famous author of *Psyche*, a friendship which cooled eventually, as the letters suggest. Other school chums and friends that figure in the correspondence are Freiherr Karl von Gersdorff, who was a student at the renowned school of Pforta together with Nietzsche, and Hermann Mushacke.

Of Nietzsche's colleagues at Basel we must mention, first of all, Franz Overbeck, a professor of church history who was somewhat incongruously one of his best admirers and faithful friends all his life. He suffered keenly when he saw disaster ahead with Nietzsche's sister acquiring exclusive publishing rights of her brother's literary productions. The other, older colleague, was Jacob Burckhardt, the historian, whose somewhat distant, timid friendship was, nevertheless, greatly treasured by Nietzsche who wrote him one of the last letters, one of the so-called *Wahnsinnszettel*, the insane notes scribbled between January 3 and 7, 1889, when, after his collapse in the *Piazza Carlo Alberto* of Turin on January 3rd his mind began to fail. Wilhelm Vischer-Bilfinger, a classical philologist and the President of the Pedagogical Institute in Basel, was a good acquaintance rather than a friend.

Dr. Paul Rée was the anonymous author of a booklet on *Psychological Observations* which endeared him to Nietzsche who, some allege, was influenced by this Jewish freethinker. Later productions of his were less favorably received by Nietzsche. Rée's intimate friend was Lou von Salomé whom Nietzsche thought, erroneously, Jewish also and with whom he had a complete meeting of minds which did not, however, lead to marriage, as he had fervently hoped. Another marriage proposal, to Mathilde Trampedach, had miscarried earlier, in 1876, but the wounds had healed more quickly than in 1882 when complications arose through Nietzsche's sister's suspicions which may have been justified, and actions which were not. At any rate, these incidents show that Nietzsche had quite normal desires which is also proven by the following story.[4]

It was on his trip from Genoa to Milan that he met a "very pleasant young ballerina" with whom he talked all the while:

> "*Camilla era molto simpatica*. Oh, you should have heard me talk Italian! Had I been a pasha I would have taken her along to Pfäfers where she could have danced before me, all intellectual diversions failing. Now and then I am still a bit angry at myself that I did not stay at least a couple of days in Milan on her account."

Heinrich Köselitz, whom Nietzsche called Peter Gast, was a musician who regarded himself a faithful disciple of Nietzsche's and who, in turn, set great store by his compositions which, however, did not find much favor with the public. He proved to be the master's most loyal friend and would have accomplished the collection, and publication, of Nietzsche's writings had not Elisabeth stayed his hand to his and Overbeck's chagrin and sorrow.

The Baroness Malwida von Meysenbug, author of *Mémoires d'une Idéaliste,* which was published in Basel, became a very good though somewhat motherly oblivious friend, and a large correspondence

10

passed between her and Nietzsche. She was apprised of many of the upheavals in Nietzsche's life, but as a Wagner enthusiast she became estranged at last as so many others who had held out in their friendship until it became a matter of choosing between Wagner and Nietzsche.

Dr. Carl Fuchs was an organist, pianist and music critic who, though apparently intrigued with Nietzsche lacked the courage to defend Nietzsche who resented his fawning: "Dr. Fuchs has again praised me flatulently in the *Wochenblatt*, which nauseates me. I am sick of him."[5]

Since the letters are replete with references to Nietzsche's illnesses, a word or two about them may be in order. As a youth he suffered from frequent headaches and excessive nearsightedness. The school authorities attributed it to a weakness inherited from his father. While in military service he fell from his horse, injuring himself. When on duty as a medical orderly, he contracted diphtheria and dysentery. Later, in Köln, he was infected with lues.[6] Insanity set in on the day already mentioned and he remained in a progressive paralytic state till the end, which occurred in 1900.

To correlate Nietzsche's philosophy with his pathological condition or even to disqualify his contributions because of it would require, it seems, on the part of those holding such a view that a philosopher first legitimize himself by showing us a clean bill of health, perhaps tell us what he has habitually for breakfast. Again, the letters, better in a way than the published books, show us a man who bore up under great suffering superbly. He wrote to friend Gustav Krug from Basel:[7]

"Sadness is not for man, but for animals, says Sancho Panza. But if one should reflect too much on it, he is becoming an animal in the process. I am avoiding now as much as I can this "animal trend" in music. Pain also must be enshrouded in such a glory of dithyrambic enchantment that it drowns in it, as it were . . ."

In the letter to Wagner containing birthday wishes[8] we read:

"True, beloved Master, to write to you at your birthday means just this: To wish *ourselves* good luck, wish *ourselves* health in order to be able to share you fully. For I am obliged to hold the opinion that it is being ill, and the egoism lurking in the sickness, which compel us to continually think of ourselves. The genius, however, in the fullness of his health, thinks always and only of others, blessing and healing without conscious effort wherever he lays his hands. Recently I read every sick person is a scoundrel,—and what all does not ail man? . . ."

A whole philosophy is contained in the following passage from a letter to Peter Gast,[9] his dearest friend whom he permitted many a look into his deeper being:

"For the purpose of fortifying myself on my life's path which I have chosen, I jotted down on yesterday, for my own purpose, a lot of traits in which I scent 'gentility' or 'nobility' in people and, contrariwise, all that belongs to the 'rabble' in us. (In all my illnesses I feel, with alarm, a sort of being dragged down to the weaknesses of the rabble, the indulgences of the rabble, even the virtues of the rabble. Do you understand that, oh, you healthy man?) Noble is, for instance, the unchanging appearance of *frivolity* by means of which a stoical severity and self-control are being *disguised*. Noble is proceeding slowly in all things, also the slow glance. Admiration with us becomes difficult. There are not too many valuable things, and these come by themselves and *desire* to tend toward us. Noble is going out of the way of petty honors and distrust of him who lauds readily. Noble is doubting that the heart can communicate. Solitude should be considered not as elected, but as given. Furthermore, the conviction is noble that one has duties only against those like us and should behave toward others as one sees fit. Noble is that one always is in the mood of *bestowing* honors while conceding to anyone on rare occasions only that he has special honors to distribute to us; that one lives nearly always in disguise, travels as it were incognito in order to save oneself much shamefacedness; that one is capable of *otium* and not like chickens diligently cackles, lays eggs, cackles again and so forth . . ."

Too much has already been written about Nietzsche and Christianity. Let the letters shed whatever light they may on this problem. They should, of course, be taken only as supporting evidence and biographical background for his published views, for, after all, what he allowed to be printed he had selected with care and wanted to be identified with. But it is his relation to Germany and the Germans which deserves another look at this time, because it is here where the dialectic, for which he had so little use, comes strikingly to the fore.

We must understand, first of all, Nietzsche's training which was in the best of German literary tradition. He was a philologist. He wrote much and worked hard over what he wrote. He had ambitions to become the finest writer of German and was persuaded that he had surpassed the best of them. His style is rhythmic, melodic (to the choice of vowels, as he himself maintained), and virile. It was for the lack of virility that he criticized Goethe, for the lack of polish and grace, Martin Luther. His own language Nietzsche appraised as "bold and German."[10] ". . . At last I myself am now the only refined *German* stylist."[11] We are not sure whether "refined" should be translated as we have it or as "cunning." Both make sense. He took pride in having coined words, such as *Bildungsphilister* which have gained general currency.

Compare with Nietzsche's style the style of German scholarly productions and the style of books written then as now without regard to the niceties of language. Of course he, like ourselves, would be pained to read them or lay them aside unread, being sensitive to language as to music. Nietzsche himself had even gone further and had dispensed with the scholarly apparatus when he wrote *The Birth of Tragedy.* Whether he was justified or not, it certainly was then as it is now a major offense in the eyes of the scholarly world. Clarity of style, in general, is related to simplicity and lack of interminable subordination within a sentence, long participial constructions and the like. By avoiding all this Nietzsche did approach English and French usage and thus acquired a taste, particularly for French. Wagner told him at one time that he wrote Latin, and he was pleased to hear it.[12]

Nietzsche's readership in Germany before he was mentally enveloped in darkness was pitifully small. Most of his published books he gave away. People were not ready to digest his message. He followed too closely upon Schopenhauer, and Schopenhauer had only very recently been appreciated by wider circles. And Nietzsche went way beyond Schopenhauer in unorthodoxy. It was a foregone conclusion that he would draw bad or at the most cautious reviews and lose the timid and the religious among his friends. But this situation only contributed to making him even more obstinate and bolder. He became persuaded more and more of what he had read in the Buddhist *Sutta Nipāta,* that he would have to "walk alone like a rhinoceros."[13]

> "My trip to Germany this summer, an interruption of my absolutely profound loneliness, has taught and frightened me. I found the entire German beast lunging against me,—I am, to tell the truth, no longer 'moral enough' for them."

Thus in a letter to Hans von Bülow.[14] He grumbled to Peter Gast that Wagner "had taken into his camp all those people in Germany whom it would have made sense to influence at all," that is, in Nietzsche's favor. In that same letter[15] he noted with satisfaction that his writings were selling better and that "even a member of the *Reichstag* and follower of Bismarck (Delbrück) had expressed his extreme displeasure over the fact that I do not live—in *Berlin,* but in Santa Margherita instead!!"

Nevertheless, his uncomplimentary remarks against

his erstwhile fellow countrymen, especially during the period in which he was writing and which was seething with political activity could not help but attract Germany's critics and enemies. With them he found *recognition* sooner than with the Germans. This did not mean, of course, as he had fondly hoped that these other nationals—French, Russians, Scandinavians, even Americans—would be his *torch bearers*, and disciples. He wanted "to press mankind to make decisions which would lay down the entire future" in a sort of blueprint.[16] But his supporters in foreign lands had no mind or heart for such decisions. They relished the negative aspect of his teachings, the anti of his criticism. In harboring false ideas about any support from this quarter Nietzsche was the victim, without knowing, of a self-deception. The almost rabid national self-criticism can never be compensated by a flight into cosmopolitanism. After all, he was neither a Swiss, though he had acquired citizenship for the sake of convenience, nor was he a Pole, though the mother of his grandfather "was a Pole yet," as he wished Heinrich von Stein to know. His claim of being a "good European" may even be doubted. Interesting is his own characterization which we find in a letter to Peter Gast.[17] The topic was his *Hymn to Life*, a musical composition: "It is something for *Germans*, a little bridge by which, perhaps, this ponderous race could reach the point of conceiving an interest in one of their oddest miscarriages."

The issue at stake was even at his time complicated by two other factors with international overtones. One was his aversion toward Catholicism as a form of overstatism, which manifested itself in him as a deeper appreciation of the principles involved in Protestantism. The other was anti-Semitism which reached its high mark around 1880. He was convinced of the wrongness of it. Occasional outbursts against Jews are met with in the correspondence, but usually they are directed against individuals like Rée. Nietzsche's sister, of all people, had to marry an outspoken anti-Semite. To the Jew Georg Morris Brandes (born Cohen) Nietzsche was grateful because it was he who popularized his name in packed lectures in Denmark; still it did not make him blind against his shortcomings which he related to Carl Fuchs.[18] One was his "passionate antipathy toward all present-day Germans" which Nietzsche did not approve of despite his own rantings. He was well aware that Brandes had made an exception to his feelings by lecturing and writing about him, a "German" scholar.

Professing such tolerance of and having defended the Jews it was, indeed, odd that Nietzsche's name served both sides, anti-Semitism and anti-anti-Semitism. The latter tendency, in so far as it manifested itself particularly outside Germany during the periods of both World Wars, did not seek, strangely enough, its basis in Nietzsche's broad views, but used his philosophical concepts of "will to power," "philosophizing with the hammer," and related thoughts to discredit him as a teacher of Germany or any other country for that matter. In other words, Nietzsche's words were exploited in a propaganda sense in Germany on the basis of "reinterpretations" for which Elisabeth Förster-Nietzsche set the precedent, and outside Germany by others who had only a superficial knowledge of Nietzsche's work, in both cases Nietzsche being in the middle and incapable of answering any.

In this connection it should be noted that among

Nietzsche scholars and popularizers we find a good number of Jews, which we should not expect on the assumption of current popular conceptions of Nietzschean philosophy and ethics. Other than the familiar Brandes and Rée we should mention Raoul Richter, Paul Mongré (pseudonym for Felix Hausdorff), Max Brahn, K. Eisner, Henri Lichtenberger, Daniel Halévy, Georg Simmel, Oskar Ludwig Levy, Julius Wilhelm Kaftan, Karl Joël, Moritz Kronenberg, Ludwig Stein, Henry Louis Mencken, and Leo Shestov-Schwartzmann who has been called the Nietzsche of Russia. The list could be extended, of course, by adding more recent names.

By way of conclusion let us say then that the letters represent valuable source material for establishing the human character of Nietzsche in its non-stereotyped aspects and may prove of worth in re-evaluating Nietzsche's ultimate thought and goals. It was he who complained that so few, if any, understood *um was es sich handelt*, "what it is all about." Though impatient and disappointed in general over the lack of interest in his message, he was, nevertheless, courteously sympathetic if his friends failed to realize "what it was all about." Study, for instance, the melancholic tone of his letter to Erwin Rohde which he wrote on November 11, 1887: ". . . You never said a word which would lead me to suspect that you *know* what destiny rests upon me."

This is the same Nietzsche who projected himself into Zarathustra, the one who steals away from Wagner and from Bayreuth in order not to court the chance of harsh words escaping his mouth when talking to his friends, the one who packs his trunk to avoid scenes at home, no doubt provoked by the

Llama and made worse by the mother who still remembered that her spouse was a Christian minister, the same who, on occasion, confessed that "the barrel of a pistol was a source of relatively pleasant thoughts."[19]

Nietzsche would not easily accuse others in the matter of misunderstanding him. He took the responsibility upon himself: ". . . It is I who made of all the incidents cruelties towards myself."[20] In all his dealings with people he maintained he was wearing a mask.[21] "I for my part am suffering abominably if I get no sympathy."[22]

". . . Even now, after an hour's agreeable conversation with total strangers, my whole philosophy is tottering. It seems so foolish to me to wish to be right for the price of love and *not to be able to communicate* what I hold most valuable in order not to destroy the sympathetic feeling. *Hinc meae lacrimae.*"[23]

Nietzsche was "not hard enough" to maintain a state of affairs which would not have permitted him to receive letters from home any longer. "Every scornful word which is written against Rée and Miss Salomé makes my heart bleed. It seems I am poorly made for enmity (while my sister wrote not long ago I should be of good cheer,—is it not a 'hale and happy war')."[24]

The "Great Noonday" of Nietzsche's is a mythologizing conception of the first magnitude and many writers have occupied themselves with it with varying success.[25] It is certainly not within our scope to explain this concept, but it is around it that Nietzsche's spiritual biography develops. Without, then, going into the deeper meaning of the song that forms the end of *Beyond Good and Evil,* let us cull the more prosaic, sober passages as a transition to the letters. The poem is largely a conversation of Nietzsche with his *alter ego* rather than a mere self-analysis or confession.

Oh noon of life! Oh solemn time!
    Oh summery garden!
Uneasy, glad, while I am stopping, peering,
    waiting—
I wait for friends, by day and night prepared.
Where are you, friends? Come, 'tis time, 'tis
    time! . . .

—Friends, there you are!—Alas! It is not *I*
    To whom you tend?
Irresolute you gape. Oh, rather growl!
I am no longer he? Changed hands, pace,
    countenance?
And what I *am*, I'm not to you, my friends?

Another I became? Strange e'en to me?
    Escaped myself?
A wrestler who too often floored himself,
Too often fought against the strength he owns,
Wounded and checked in his own victory?

Did I not search where gales most violent blow?
    Did I not learn to dwell
Where no one lives, in dreary regions of the polar
    bear,
Forgetting man and god, and prayer and curse?
Did I become a phantom walking over glaciers?

Lo! Friends of old! Your countenance is pale,
  Love-filled, but shuddering!
Nay off! Allay your anger! Here *you* could not
    dwell,
Here 'twixt farthest ice and rocky regions—
Here hunter must you be and chamois-like.

You turn away?—Oh, heart you bore enough,
  But valiant hope remained.
For *new* friends keep the doors wide open!
Let go of old ones! Leave memory behind!
If young you were one time—now are you better
    young!
    . . .
Whoever changes, he alone remains my kin.
Oh noon of life! My second youth!
  Oh summery garden!
Uneasy, glad, while I am stopping, peering,
    waiting!
I wait for friends, by day and night prepared.
For *new* friends! Come, 'tis time, 'tis time.
. . .

K. F. L.

NOTES

1. Cf. the passage on page 88 of Karl Schlechta: *Der Fall Nietzsche* (Carl Hanser Verlag, München, 1958).

2. Carl Hanser Verlag, München. Volume 1 (1954), 1279 pp.; volume 2 (1955), 1267 pp.; volume 3 (1956), 1472 pp.

3. Letter of July 25, 1882.

4. Letter to Malwida von Meysenbug of May 13, 1877.

5. Letter to Erwin Rohde, March 19, 1874.

6. More about this in Walter Kaufmann: *Nietzsche. Philosopher, Psychologist, Antichrist* (Meridian Books, N. Y., 1958 printing), p. 366-367.

7. December 31, 1871.

8. Dated Basel, May 24, 1875.

9. Dated Sils-Maria, July 23, 1885.

10. Letter to Carl Fuchs, December 14, 1887.

11. Letter to Malwida von Meysenbug, October 4, 1888.

12. Letter to Heinrich von Stein, beginning December 1882.

13. Letter to Carl von Gersdorff, December 13, 1875.

14. December 1882, written from near Genoa.

15. From Rapallo, February 19, 1883.

16. Letter to Malwida von Meysenbug, written in May 1884 from Venice.

17. October 27, 1887.

18. Letter of August 26, 1888, written in Sils.

19. Letter to Franz Overbeck, written from Rapallo and received February 11, 1883.

20. *Ibid.*

21. *Ibid.*

22. Letter to Peter Gast, August 20, 1880.

23. *Ibid.*

24. Letter to Franz Overbeck written in summer 1883 from Sils-Maria. Similarly in another letter to him from Nice, April 7, 1884: ". . . Dr. Rée and Miss Salomé, to whom I would like to make up what my sister has done to them in harm."

25. An excellent treatise is Karl Schlechta: *Nietzsches Grosser Mittag* (Vittorio Klostermann, Frankfurt a. M., 1954).

THE LETTERS

(1) To Elisabeth Nietzsche

(Pforta, end of November 1861)
From your brother

Dear Liese:—Since I owe you a letter for quite some time I shall write you an especially fine one now, provided my clumsy pen will not prevent me. Probably there is nothing with which I can entertain you now except writing of—Christmas. Anyhow, isn't it now our best-loved thought and hasn't it been all these years around this time! Now, then, lean back comfortably and try to recall one of my first evenings of vacation when we were sitting in the warm room with or without lamp light, and each would present the other with a Christmas list. Meanwhile Mamma and aunt Rosalie would engage next door in mysterious doings and

     —we eavesdrop
when secretly words pass between them;
and a rustling, quite peculiar,
now a whisper, now a crackling,
make us curious for the wonders,
while the ghostlike stirring
and the wafting to and fro
make us tremble etc.

I hope you have not made your list so definitive that I may not at least give you the benefit of a few suggestions. I wrote down quite a number of desirable books and sheets of music and would like to tell you about some. Amongst the latter, for instance, a work by Schumann seems to me to be rather suitable for you, the same Schumann who composed the broken window pane.

I am sure it represents his most beautiful songs in general; it is *Frauenliebe und Leben,* poems by Chamisso, and should cost around 20 *Silbergroschen.* The text also is absolutely beautiful. Among books I could recommend, first of all, two works on theology which will interest both you and me very much. I myself heard them praised by Wenkel himself which, I take it, is significant as far as you are concerned. Both works are by Hase, the famous professor who lives in Jena. He is the most keen-witted champion of ideal rationalism, whose lectures I almost came to attend at one time. *The Life of Jesus* (1.6) is one of the works and Church History (2.6) is the other. Both are or, rather, each singly is 1 *Taler* and 15 *Silbergroschen.* Write me if you want to have the correct address. Or would you rather have an English book? If I were in your place I would most decidedly read Byron in English. The book costs 1 *Taler* and 25 *Silbergroschen.* I could jot down a number of different books for you. Presently I will give you my list.

Now, as concerns music I like to have *Paradies und die Peri* by Schumann in the solo arrangement for piano. That is something that delights everybody and would delight you also. Next, Shelley's poetical works translated by Seybt. Schumann costs about 2 *Talers* if you get it through Gustav, Shelley is 1

Taler and 10 *Silbergroschen*. I would be beside myself with joy were I given both, for this is all I want.

By the way, I am just reminded of something I
have to tell you. Last Sunday noon I was invited to
Dr. Heinze's for a meal. The food was very good but
the conversation was still more delectable. Moreover,
the new teacher, Dr. Volkmann, is prepared to give
private lessons in English. Lots of people have applied. As for me, however, I shall join not until Easter.
At the moment I am still studying Italian privately,
as you know. I am taking Latin, Greek, and Hebrew
in which we are reading *Genesis*. In German we read
the *Nibelungenlied* in the original, in French we read
Karl XII in class and *Athalie* in a group of three, ex-
cluding me. In Italian I am reading Dante with a
group. If that is not enough for the present, then I
do not know, especially since in Latin we are simultaneously reading Virgil, Livius, Cicero and Hero-
dotus.—For now farewell and hope you are enjoying
this rather long epistle.

Until we meet again on Sunday in Almrich
                                    Your Fritz

(2) To Franziska Nietzsche

(Pforta, probably May 2, 1863)

Dear Mamma:—Your dear letter with the caramel for
the chest was very much appreciated, especially since
you informed me about quite a few things in which,
as you know, I am much interested. Let me report,
first of all, about my being indisposed. My hoarseness

is still present and, to be sure, without relief. Since yesterday I am drinking Seltzer water with milk which seems to be giving me some relief. By and by I am getting the blues in this sickroom, particularly today as the weather is fine and the sky is laughing. Even though I am at work I do not accomplish much because I am lacking one or the other book. I am making extracts from Hettner's *History of Literature of the Eighteenth Century* and, in general, am much occupied with the history of literature.

Concerning my future I am a little disturbed by some very practical considerations. The decision as to what I should specialize in does not come to me out of thin air. I have got to think about it myself and arrive at a choice. It is this choice which bothers me. Certainly it is my endeavor to study thoroughly whatever I am going to study; but the choice is all the more difficult inasmuch as one has to ferret out that field in which one can hope to accomplish something worth-while. And how deceptive do one's expectations turn out quite often! How easy it is to be carried away by some ephemeral preference, or some old family tradition, or by some special desires. Choosing, thus, a profession is much like playing the lottery with its great number of blanks and mighty few hits. Now, I am also in the rather inconvenient position to have really a great number of interests which are distributed over different fields and which, if I were to follow through with all of them, would make me a learned man, but hardly a professional person in the narrow sense. I am clear in my own mind that I must, therefore, slough off a few interests and, by the same token, add a few new ones. However, which are the unlucky ones I shall have to throw overboard? Perhaps they are the very ones that are my favorites!

I cannot speak more plainly. It is evident the situation is critical and I have to arrive at a decision in the coming year. It will not come automatically, and as for me I know too little about the different fields.

Enough of this.—Really I have nothing further to write about, except that I am very sorry that I did not get to see the married couple in Pforta.

Give my greetings to Lisbeth and uncle.

The best to you all

Fritz

(3) To Franziska and Elisabeth Nietzsche

(Bonn, October 24 and 25, 1864)
Monday morning

Dear Mamma and Lisbeth:—Most courteous bows to the right and to the left: introducing myself to you as a member of the German student fraternity Franconia!

Now, I can see with my mind's eye how you people are shaking your heads in a most peculiar manner, giving forth with a cry of astonishment. There are, indeed, many wonderful things connected with this step and, therefore, I shall not blame you. For instance, almost at the same time that I joined the Franconia seven men from Pforta did so and, to be sure, all of them, except two, not only came from Pforta but met in Bonn. Among them are many who are already in their fourth semester. I shall name you some whom you may know: Deussen, Stöckert, Haushalter, Töpelmann, Stedefeld, Schleussner, Michael, and myself.

Of course, I gave mature reflection to the step before I took it and have come to the conclusion that in view of what I am it was almost necessary. For the most part we are all philologists and at the same time music lovers. In general, a very interesting spirit is prevailing in the Franconia, and I liked the older men immensely.

Before joining I became intimately acquainted also with the Marchia and elected some for more intimate intercourse. I also inspected the Germania fraternity so that I was quite qualified to make a comparison which, however, turned out in favor of Franconia.

Until now I have experienced on all hands much that is pleasant and dear. The other day I paid a visit to Brambach, the music conductor, and let him make me a member of the municipal choral society. I accompanied some of the men from Brandenburg on a trip to Rolandseck. The country is beautiful and we enjoyed beautiful days. Yesterday the Franconia brothers went to Plittersdorf where a kermess was going on. We danced a lot and drank cider at a peasant's. In the evening I went with a brother from the Franconia, my orderly, whom I like especially well, along the Rhine back to Bonn. On the hills the vintagers had lit their fires. You would not believe how beautiful everything was.

Recently I was greatly pleased to meet the dear Baron of Frankenstein by accident and visit with him for a couple of hours at Hotel Kley. He is the very same amiable person as before. He enquired interestedly about you and conditions in Naumburg. He intends to pay me a visit one of these days. Hachtmann also looked me up. I am going to call on Dr. Wachsmuth today.

Also today I shall go to the cemetery in order to pay a visit to the graves of Schumann, Schlegel and Arndt. In the afternoon I shall go with my landlord and landlady to a neighboring village for a kermess. They are very nice and pleasant people who take care of me in a way I should find satisfying all-around. My lodgings are most delightful, I eat very well, am waited upon neatly and punctually, and am happy to spend an hour in the evening with them.

Just now I returned from the marvelous cemetery where I laid a wreath on Schumann's grave. My landlady and her niece, Miss Marie (everybody on the Rhine is called Marie) accompanied me.

Now, dear Lisbeth, a special message to you: Our colors are white-red-gold, our caps are white with a red-gold border. Furthermore, I want to introduce to you some old Bonn brothers of the Franconia as old acquaintances: Max Rötger (truffle sausage) and Treitzschke who distinguished himself as speaker at the Leipzig meeting of gymnasts, Fritz Spielhagen whom you may recall quite well because of his "In the Twelfth Hour," which is playing in Bonn. In general, the Franconia has a very fine name.

The university lectures have not begun yet. The other day I received a present from Pastor Kletschke, a book entitled *Jesus' Freedom from Sin*, by Ullmann, together with an extremely cordial letter in which he signs off with "Cordially yours, your friend." I was very happy over this interesting book. I presume he has called on you.

The coffee maker supplies me now every morning with a very good cup of coffee and I thank the giver, ever so dear to me, from my heart. I now anticipate most anxiously receiving my box and above all letters from you from which I can gauge the effect the step I have taken has made on you. Please convey my cordial greetings to aunt Rosalie and to anyone who is interested in me.

The very best to you

Fritz

Dear Lisbeth:—Should Mrs. Anna Redtel still be in Kösen, deign to convey my respects to her and tell her that whenever I sip my coffee in Hotel Kley in view of the magnificent Siebengebirge, I speed greetings to her.

Tuesday evening. I received the box and am greatly pleased over it, especially the nice linen things and the beautiful music literature. Yesterday we enjoyed a most jolly afternoon. I danced fabulously.

I am always taking my meals together with Deussen in my room. We have reason to be quite contented. I look well and vigorous and am always rather moderate. I registered for theology and philosophy. Dr. Wachsmuth has received a call as professor at Marburg. I am the owner of a pretty petroleum lamp.

(4) To Elisabeth Nietzsche

Bonn, Sunday after Whitsuntide
(June 11, 1865)

Dear Lisbeth:—After so charming a letter inter-twined with girlish poetry as I received from you lately it would be injustice combined with ingratitude to let you wait still longer for an answer, especially since I now have rich material at my disposal and am "ruminating" mentally, but with great gusto, the delights I have experienced.

First of all, however, I have to touch upon a passage in your letter which you wrote alike with pastoral hues and llamalike cordiality. Don't be trou-bled, dear Lisbeth. If your determination is so good and firm as you write me, the dear uncles won't have too much difficulty. As far as your principle is concerned according to which truth is always on the side of what is difficult, I admit this is true. Nonetheless it is not easy to comprehend that 2 x 2 should not be 4. Is it truer on that account?

Is it really so difficult to accept simply and straightforwardly all one has been educated for, all that has gradually taken deep roots and is looked upon as truth in the circles of relatives and many good folks, and, moreover, is consoling and uplifting people? But, considering things contrariwise, is ac-cepting all this more difficult than striking out on new paths in conflict with custom, uncertain of one's step when walking independently, shifting one's moods frequently, indeed, one's conscience, lacking often all comfort but always having the eternal goal of the True, the Beautiful and the Good in view?

Is it, then, a matter of arriving at a concept of

God, world and atonement which will give us the feeling of greatest snugness? The true seeker, does he not rather treat the result of his search as something to be considered almost with indifference? When exploring are we looking for rest, peace, happiness? No, only truth, even if it were most repelling and ugly.

One final question: Supposing we had believed since our youth that the welfare of our souls stems in its entirety from another person but Jesus, flows from, let us say, Mohammed. Would we not be sure we had partaken of the same blessings? I am certain, faith alone blesses, not the object of faith. I am writing you this, dear Lisbeth, only in order thus to counter the commonest proofs the believing give us who appeal to their inner experiences and derive the infallibility of their faith from it. Every true faith is, indeed, infallible. It accomplishes what the pious person in question hopes to find in it; but it offers not the least support for a basis of objective truth.

It is here that the paths of men part. Should you long for peace of soul and happiness? Then by all means believe. Should you want to become a disciple of truth? Then search.

In between there are numerous points of view which are taken halfheartedly. The important thing is the main goal ahead.

Please forgive me for this boring discourse which is not exactly brilliant. You have probably said this many times and every time better and more beautifully.

But now I want to rear a more cheerful structure on this serious foundation. This time I can give you a report on wonderful days.

On Friday, June 2nd, I travelled to Köln this

side of the river to attend the Lower Rhenish Music Festival. The international exposition was opening the same day. Köln in those days made a cosmopolitan impression. An interminable tangle of languages and costumes, an immense number of pickpockets and other swindlers, all hotels full even to their remotest rooms, the city most charmingly decorated with flags,—that was the outward picture. As a vocalist they gave me a white and red silken ribbon for my chest and thus decked out I strutted to the rehearsal. Unfortunately, you are not acquainted with the Gürzenich Hall. However, I can give you a fabulous idea by comparing it with the stock-exchange in Naumburg which I described to you during my last vacation.

Our choir was composed of 182 sopranos, 154 altos, 113 tenors, and 172 basses. In addition, there was an orchestra consisting of some 160 artists, among them 52 violins, 20 violas, 21 violoncellos, and 14 double basses. Seven of the best vocal soloists, men and women, had been engaged. Hiller directed the whole. Amongst the ladies many distinguished themselves by youth and beauty. They all came in white during the three main concerts, with blue ribbons passing under their arms and natural or artificial flowers in their hair. Each carried a pretty bouquet in her hand. We gentlemen wore tails and a white vest.

On the first evening we sat together far into the night and I went to sleep at last in the reclining chair at an old brother's of the Franconia. In the morning I was totally crimped like a pocket knife. I may add in passing that ever since my last vacation I am suffering from a sharp rheumatic pain in my left arm. The following night I passed again at Bonn. Sunday was the day of the first great concert, Hän-

del's "Israel in Egypt." We sang with inimitable enthusiasm at a temperature of 50 degrees Réaumur.
Gürzenich Hall was sold out on all three days. Single
admission per concert was two to three *Talers*. The
performance was perfect, so everybody said. Scenes
took place which I shall never forget. When Staege-
mann and Julius Stockhausen, "the King of Basses,"
had finished their famous heroic duet, a storm of
jubilation broke loose never heard ere this. There
were shouts of eightfold bravos, trumpet flourishes,
yells of *da capo*, and all of the 300 ladies flung their
300 bouquets into the singers' faces so that they were
literally buried in a flowery cloud. The scene was
repeated when the duet was sung a second time.

As we men from Bonn began later in the evening
to drink a glass of beer together, we were invited
by the Köln Male Choir to the Gürzenich Restaurant.
There we stayed together, toasting each other and
singing just like at a carnival in which the people
of Köln excel. We sang in four voices and enthusiasm
was rising as time went on. With two acquaintances
I stole away at 3 o'clock in the morning. We went
through the city ringing door bells, but found no
place to stay in, even the post office did not offer us
accommodation (we wanted to sleep in the mail
vans), until finally after an hour and a half a night
watchman unlocked the *Hôtel du Dome*. We slumped
on to the benches of the dining hall and within two
seconds were fast asleep. Outside day was breaking.
In an hour and a half the porter arrived and awakened us inasmuch as the hall was to be cleaned.
Desperate in mind, but full of fun, we got up, went
by way of the station across the river to Deutz, enjoyed breakfast and with voices quite damped went
to rehearsal where with immense enthusiasm I fell

asleep, trombones and kettledrums furnishing the *obbligato*.

I was all the more awake, however, during the performance in late afternoon, from 6 to 11 o'clock. Did I not hear those pieces which I loved most,— Schumann's Faust music and Beethoven's Symphony in A-major? In the evening I longed very much for a place to rest and went around to some thirteen hotels, all being full and more than full. Finally, in the fourteenth, and even though the proprietor had assured me as elsewhere that all rooms were occupied, I drew myself up and simply stated in cold blood that I would remain, let him take care to provide a bed. He did, indeed, and they put army cots in one of the dining rooms for which he asked 20 *Groschen* per night.

On the third day, at last, the final concert took place. It included the production of a larger number of smaller items. The most beautiful moment of them all occurred when they were playing Hiller's symphony with the motto "Spring is bound to come." The musicians were in a state of rare enthusiasm, for we all venerate Hiller deeply. After every part there were tremendous shouts of joy and after the last one there was a similar scene, only more climactic. The conductor's platform was covered with wreaths and bouquets, one of the virtuosos put a laurel wreath upon his head, the orchestra struck up a threefold flourish, and the old man covered his face and wept. This moved the ladies immensely.

One lady in especial I would like to mention to you, Mrs. Szarvadi from Paris, a virtuosa at the piano. Picture to yourself a petite, still youthful personality, full of fire, lacking in beauty, stimulating, her hair in black locks.

Due to total absence of *nervus rerum* I spent the last night again at the Franconia brotherhood and, to be sure, on the floor. This was not very agreeable. In the morning I rode back to Bonn.

One lady said to me, "this was leading the life of pure art."

One might say it is with complete irony that one returns to his books, textual criticism, and stuff like that.

My return to Leipzig is certain. The dispute between Jahn and Ritschl continues unabated. Both parties use the threat of devastating publications. Deussen may likewise go to Leipzig.

As students at Bonn from Pforta we dispatched a telegram to the faculty on the occasion of the academic celebrations on the 21st of May and received a very friendly answer.

Today we Pforta scholars are having an outing at Königswinter.—Our captains in red look splendid with their golden braid.

I intend to write not too long hence to dear Rudolf who sent me such a cordial letter. Please remember me affectionately to our dear aunt and uncle.

Fritz

(5) To Hermann Mushacke

Naumburg, Wednesday
(August 30, 1865)

My dear Friend:—As much as I enjoyed reading
every item in your exceedingly kind letter, I was
annoyed at myself for not being able to do what you
asked of me, which was only fair and just. Please
try and picture my situation to you. I used up more
money than I should have, much more, in fact. I must
avoid the least suggestion that I still have debts so
as not to render my position untenable. Thus, I am
placed in the desperate situation to be obliged to
write you truly shamefacedly that I am "not able."
And, besides, what a miserable sum which is involved!

Nevertheless, I cannot square myself with the
thought that I may not have acted as a friend should
in writing you this. I will not blame you were you
to become angry with me. But now enough of this.

Perhaps, you are able to find an explanation why
I think back to Bonn with somewhat unpleasant feelings. True, I still am much too close to the things
and moods I experienced there. The bitter shell of
the present, of reality, prevents me from getting to
the enjoyment of the core. For I hope that when
I think back on these experiences I shall be able
to mark down this year also cheerfully as a necessary
link in my development. For the moment, I cannot
do that. The thought haunts me still that I may have
squandered away this year with mistakes in many
directions. My having remained in the fraternity, I
must openly confess, seems to have been a *faux pas;*
I am thinking of the last summer semester. I went

back on my principle which is, not to devote myself to things and humans beyond the time I have come to know them thoroughly.

The punishment for this follows as a matter of course. I am annoyed with myself. This feeling has somewhat spoiled my summer and even clouded my objective judgment of the fraternity. I am not one who is an unconditional partisan to Franconia. I could very easily picture myself a more amiable society. Its political judgment I deem quite low and residing merely in the heads of a few. Its appearance in public I find plebeian and repulsive. Since I did not hold back very much with my unfavorable criticism my position with respect to my fraternity brothers was rendered uncomfortable.

In this connection I must always think with gratitude of you. How often did I not lose in your, and only in your, presence the peeved mood which dominated me most of the time. Hence the pleasant memories of good times I had in Bonn are forever connected with the picture I have of you.

In truth, I should also be dissatisfied with my studies even though I chalk much off to the account of the fraternity which thwarted my most beautiful plans. Especially these days I am aware what beneficent tranquility and exaltation are to be found in continuous and absorbing work. Such peace of mind I seldom experienced in Bonn. Scornfully I must look upon what I produced and finished there at Bonn. There is an essay for the Gustav-Adolf-Society, one for an evening at the fraternity, and one for the seminar. Detestable! I am mortified when I think of this trash. Everyone of my essays in high school was better.

In the lectures I learned nothing, some things

here and there excepted. To Springer I am indebted for *enjoyment;* I would be grateful to Ritschl had I used him diligently. In general I am not at all disappointed over all this. I set great store by self-development, but how easily can one be rendered impotent by men like Ritschl and be carried away into channels which are, perhaps, far removed from one's own inclinations.

That I have gained much toward an understanding of myself I reckon is the greatest yield of that year. And that I have won a friend who has deep sympathies, I count as no less a gain.

These things belong together so far as I am concerned. On the one hand, I think it strange that a man like myself with so many inner dissonances, with disdainful and often frivolous opinions, could have drawn such a dear person to himself; on the other hand, I draw hope from this selfsame situation. Thus, in moments when the spirit negates everything I ask myself whether my dear friend Mushacke knows me, possibly, too little.—

At this juncture let me catch my breath and write of something different. As already stated I am working assiduously. Theognis is being manhandled terribly. With a critical pair of scissors hanging by a long methodic thread, I snip off daily a few patches of tinsel. Now and then, when every path seems blocked, I feel as if I should despair over the whole investigation. If results do appear—and I can hardly afford to neglect them—they will be worked over into a paper to be presented to the seminar in Leipzig. In case Ritschl becomes director, we have preferred stock. Professor Steinhart describes the philologists at Leipzig in a very unfavorable light. Devotion to science is not a living reality there, the people want position and income as soon as possible. Hence Ritschl cannot any longer look forward to conditions such as prevailed in Bonn. The tradition of G. Hermann is supposed to have disappeared in Leipzig without a trace. Philosophy and history are completely lacking.

Even at this moment I do not know whether my mother and sister will move with me to Leipzig. But one thing is certain that I will visit with you, beginning the first of October, and I shall do so with the greatest of joy. I shall write you more in detail by what train I shall arrive, etc.

My health is better for the time being than it was in Bonn. They thought I looked somewhat wretched and, therefore, quasi nursed me back to health by feeding me well. I avoid company. The excitability of my nerves has not yet been allayed.

Of course, I play the piano a great deal. Already at 5 o'clock in the morning I enjoy the clear, blue days of late summer, and often say to myself that I should be quite happy. Moreover, I am reading nice books, such as Laube's travel novels and beautiful letters, such as the one written by my friend Mushacke in Bonn and containing a highly humorous description of conditions there.

But, darkness is descending. I am sending you warm greetings straight from the heart into the beautiful Rhineland and hope for joyous and contented days and nights for you.

Thine

Fritz Nietzsche

(6) To Franziska and Elisabeth Nietzsche

(Leipzig, end of June, 1866)

Dear Mamma and Lisbeth:—I hope you are subscribing to a newspaper so you have been able to follow diligently what the weeks have brought in the way of decisive events. The danger to which Prussia is exposed is tremendous. It is altogether impossible for her to be able to carry out her program, leave alone by a complete victory. To found the united German state in such a revolutionary manner, is a daring feat of Bismarck's. He does possess courage and is ruthlessly consistent, but he underestimates the moral forces in the people. At any rate, his last chess moves were excellent, however. Above all, he knew how to devolve a huge, if not the major part of the blame upon the shoulders of Austria.

Our position is quite simple. If the house is on fire one does not ask first who is to be blamed for the conflagration; one puts it out. Prussia is afire. Now the problem is to salvage. That is the general feeling.

When the war began, at that moment all secondary considerations had to be put aside. I am just as much an enraged Prussian as, for instance, our cousin is a Saxon. For all Saxons, however, it is an especially grave time. Their country is entirely in enemy hands. Their army is quiet and inactive. Their king is far away from his subjects. Another king and Elector were simply done away with. This is the latest explanation of a "Principality by the Grace of God." Now you can understand when the old Gerlach, together with some Westphalian Borneos, denounce a union with the crowned (Victor Emman-[uel]) as well as uncrowned democracy.

43

In the last analysis this Prussian way of getting rid of the princes is the most convenient in the world. It must unquestionably be considered lucky that Hanover and the Electorate of Hesse did not make common cause with Prussia, otherwise we would not have gotten rid of these gentlemen for all eternity.

Thus we live in the Prussian city of Leipzig. Today they have declared the state of war throughout Saxony. Gradually you begin to feel as if you were living on an island inasmuch as telegraphic dispatches, the postal system and the railroads are continually interrupted. Of course, to Naumburg all connections are intact, as in general they are to Prussia. But to send a letter, for instance, to Deussen in Tübingen is hardly possible.

In all this turmoil the university lectures continue without disturbance. Recently when I returned from Naumburg I found a letter from Ritschl in which he told me of the arrival of the Roman collation. The one from Paris will arrive end of the week.

Nevertheless, I am constantly aware that the day is very near on which I shall be called up. Withal it would be patently dishonorable were I to sit at home when the Fatherland is about to engage in a life-and-death struggle. Please go to the county seat and get absolutely reliable information regarding the time when those enlisting for one year only are going to be called up, and let me know posthaste.

The most delectable thing Leipzig still offers is Hedwig Raabe who continues to play to sold-out houses at a time when the Dresden theatre, for example, took in only six *Talers*.

So long for today. Let me have soon again laundry and news. I send you hearty greetings.

F. W. N.

Continuation

Since this letter was not sent you will hardly get furious if you receive a postscript. I was sick for three days, but today I am all right again. The heat must have impaired my health. But that is a matter of indifference. Important is, however, that our soldiers have won their first important victory. Day before yesterday our City Commandant published the news and immediately had a huge black-and-white flag hoisted at his hotel. The temper of the populace is rather divided. They believe in the wretched lies emanating from Vienna according to which all these last successful engagements meant as great a loss for Prussia. Stories circulate about taking 15,000 prisoners among the Prussians. Only fools believe that. In order to create morale among the people, all dispatches were falsified in Vienna, that we know.

Incidentally, I am extremely delighted about the brilliant bust ($\pi\alpha\pi\pi\alpha\xi$) of the Naumburg-Zeitz conservatives at the last elections. We do not want any egoists in the chamber who, in furtherance of their own schemes, act hypocritically, become yesmen, crawl and burst like puffballs with their "your obedient servant." And there was a great stink.

I did get your letter with that of Gersdorff's in it and can dispel your fears. As if you were so much more secure than I am in Leipzig! For the present, I shall stay here and really would not care in these times to be pent up in a somewhat sleepy and newspaperless little dump which exudes the odor of newspapers mailed in wrappers.

For Gersdorff's oldest brother I really am concerned. The Ziethen Dragoons were in the front lines and are said to have suffered severe losses. Our Gersdorff expects to become an officer as soon as three months hence, provided stupid cadets are not promoted over him.

With this I bid you farewell. May all be well with you. When the Llama is celebrating her birthday I may be coming to Naumburg. But before that I would like to get a letter with the whole story on the induction proceedings.

F. W. N.

(7) To Paul Deussen

(Leipzig, second half of October, 1868)

My dear Friend:—Your letters arrive of late at some special festive occasion. Thus, when, not too long ago, I moved to my new residence in Leipzig, your letter which our friend Roscher had correctly dispatched here, was lying on the table. Soon thereafter I addressed the first part of my *Laertianum* to you so I may not be accused again of being ungrateful to my friends and through continuous silence create the impression as if I were dead. Nay, I live and, what's more, live well and wish that you would sometime personally convince yourself of it, especially to realize that φιλοσοφεῖν (to philosophize) and being sick are not really identical concepts, but that, on the contrary, there is a certain "health," the eternal foe of profound philosophy which, as you know, nowadays has become the nickname of certain kinds of border heroes and historians.

While continuing the thought expressed at the

end of your letter, I shall at the same time reply to the proposition you hint at. Dear friend, "being able to write well" (if I deserve this praise: *nego ac pernego*) I should think really does not justify one to write a criticism of Schopenhauer's system. Moreover, you cannot adequately conceive of the respect which I have of this "genius of the first order of magnitude" if you think *I* (i.e., *homini pusillullullo!*) have the ability to make mincemeat of said giant. For I hope you do not understand by criticism of a system merely the singling out of certain faulty passages, unsuccessful proofs, or tactic ineptitudes. Of course, certain foolhardy Ueberwegs and Hayms who are not at home in philosophy, do believe that with such a treatment everything has been done. At all events you do not write a criticism of a world view. Rather, one understands it or does not understand it; a third standpoint is unfathomable to my way of thinking. Someone who does not smell the fragrance of a rose surely should not be permitted to criticize it; and if he smells it, *à la bonheur!* he will not have the inclination to criticize it.

We simply do not understand each other. Let me be silent about the things under consideration. Does my memory serve me right if I seem to recall that I have already proposed this to you?

Concerning your refusal to apologize I am also not very much satisfied, even less so with your impression that I expected you to defend "philology." I am not in the least interested in that. But I do want to know what you are thinking concerning the present situation in philology, prevalent methods, the current training of philologists, their attitudes with respect to the schools, etc. All this I would like to know, your views being contrary to the ones I expressed somewhat harshly. For, to speak clearly (or "martially") in letters has the special advantage of making one's partner abandon a noncommittal, compromising stand and press him for a direct yea or nay. Of course, one must have reasons. But you do not furnish any, not even the slightest one, for your mythological conception of philology as the daughter (daughter, no less! *heu! heu!*) of philosophy which as such is supposed to be beyond all control and jurisdiction. Should I speak mythologically, I would say philology is the miscarriage of the Goddess Philosophy, conceived by an idiot or half-wit. Too bad Plato did not already invent the same myth for you would rather believe him, and rightfully so.—

To be sure, I ask of every individual science its passport, and if she cannot show that on her periphery lie some great cultural objectives, I shall still let her pass since the loonies have the same right to exist in the realm of knowledge as they do in the domain of life. But I have to laugh when these loony sciences pathetically act up and display the buskin. Similarly, some sciences become senile sometime or other. The spectacle is saddening when such sciences, emaciated of body, with dried-up veins and wrinkled lips, seek out the blood of young and blossoming natures and, like vampires, suck them dry. Assuredly it must be the duty of an educator to keep fresh forces from being entwined by these senile, hideous monsters who can expect deferential treatment from the historian's point of view, disgust from the present generation, and destruction by future generations.

Alla tauta men tropikos. Hemeis de, dear friend, are disciples of the present; *soyons de notre siècle!*—

Finally a couple of personal trivia. First of all, I

ask you to write me a few words about the *Laerti-anum*, because I would like to know what position such like works occupy in your *ingenium* in respect of worth. Secondly, I owe you an explanation of how, where and why I live here. Well, it is not as a student. It is more than a year that I have quit this intolerable condition. Rather, I am here, the future *Privatdozent* of Leipzig, and am systematically arranging my existence in accordance with this object in view. The family where I have made my nice home is that of Professor Biedermann, a former Member of Parliament and now editor of the *Deutsche Allgemeine*. Through him I am able to make a number of interesting acquaintances, such as smart women, pretty actresses, important authors and politicians, etc. A number of larger essays are awaiting the blessed event about which I shall write you later. Ritschl, the teacher whom I esteem, and his wife who is very close to me, show me many favors. Also, I flourish in the circle of ambitious friends and associates and only regret that I do not have around me the excellent Paul Deussen.

(8) To Carl von Gersdorff

(Naumburg, April 11, 1869)

My dear Friend:—The last day has arrived, the last evening which I am spending in my home land. Tomorrow morning I am off into the wide, wide world, into a new and unaccustomed occupation, into a grave and oppressing atmosphere of duty and work. Once again I have to take leave. The golden time of free and unhampered activity, of sovereign presence, of the enjoyment of art and the world as a nonpartici- pant or at least weakly participating spectator,—this time has irrevocably passed. Now reigns the severe goddess, daily duty. "Anciently a student I fare forth . . ." you know, of course, the touching student song. Yes, yes! Must now be Philistine myself! Some- where this sentence never loses its truth. One is never in office or occupies a place of dignity without pun- ishment,—it is only a matter of whether the shackles are of iron or of twine. I still have the courage to break a manacle on occasion and to try elsewhere and in a different manner this living precariously. I do not feel a trace yet of the professorial humpback. To be a Philistine, a man devoid of the muses, to be of the herd,—Zeus and all ye muses preserve me from this fate! Neither would I know how I should go about it to become one, since I am not of such a strain. To be sure, I have come close to a kind of Philistinism, the *species* "specialist." It is only natural that the daily load, concentrating one's thinking every hour of the day on certain fields of knowledge and problems, somewhat blunts the free receptivity and undermines the very significance of philosophy at its root. But I think I can face this danger with more composure and steadiness than most philologists. A philosophic earnestness is too deeply rooted in me, the true and essential problems of life and thought were pointed up too clearly for me by the great mystagogue Schopenhauer than that I ever should have to fear a scandalous desertion of the "Idea." To infuse into my presentation of the science this new blood, to transfer to my hearers that Schopenhauerian serious- ness which is impressed on the forehead of this grand man,—this is my desire, my audacious hope. I would like to be something more than a drillmaster of competent philologists. The present generation of teachers, nursing the growing brood,—all this is before my mental vision. If once our lives are dedicated let us try to shape them so that, should we happily have to depart, others will bless us for having been of value to them.

To you, precious friend, with whom I am at one in many of the basic questions of life I wish luck, which you deserve; to me I wish your old and loyal friendship. Until we meet again!

Friedrich Nietzsche, Dr.

I thank you cordially for your meaty letters. Please excuse me for having been so busy that I am thanking you so late. Thanks to Wieseke were dispatched by letter.

(9) To Richard Wagner

(Basel, May 22, 1869)

My dear Sir:—How long have I not had the intention for once to state frankly and unabashedly the measure of gratitude I feel toward you! In truth, the best and noblest moments of my life are linked with your name and I know only of one other man, that is, a great spirit akin to you, Arthur Schopenhauer, of whom I think with equal veneration, yes *religione quadam*. I am glad that I am able to confess thus on a festive day and I am telling you this not without a feeling of pride. For, if it is the lot of genius to be for a little while only *paucorum hominum,* these *pauci* may feel to a certain degree happy and distinguished since they have been permitted to see the light and warm themselves by it while the multitude still stands in the cold mist and freezes. Moreover, the enjoyment of genius does not fall into the lap of those few without any trouble; rather, they must fight valiantly against all-powerful prejudices and their own counterinclinations so that if the battle turns in their favor they have acquired a sort of conqueror's right in the genius.

Now I have dared to count myself among the number of those *pauci* after becoming aware how lacking in capacity almost everyone is with whom one comes in contact if it is a question of comprehending your personality as a whole, of feeling the unified, deeply ethical current which flows through your life, your writings and your music, in brief, if the problem is one of sensing the atmosphere of a more serious and soulful view of the world which we poor Germans have lost overnight by virtue of all sorts of wretched political conditions, philosophical mischief and insolent Jewry. I owe it to you and Schopenhauer if, till now, I have held fast to the Teutonic seriousness with which to look upon life, have clung to a deeper insight into this our so mysterious and hazardous existence.

I would rather relate to you sometime by word of mouth how many purely scientific problems have found their solution gradually in my mind, simply by relating them to your singular, remarkable personality. At the same time I wish that what I have just written I would not have had to *write.* How gladly would I have turned up today in your lake and mountain solitude, had it not been for the miserable chain of my profession which keeps me in my dog-house at Basel.

Finally, I would like to ask you to remember me kindly to Baroness von Bülow and crave permission to sign

Your most loyal and devoted disciple and admirer
Dr. Nietzsche, Prof. at Basel

(10) To Erwin Rohde

(Naumburg, October 7, 1869)

Hail and Blessing before!

The heading of this letter shows you what ex-uberance has been mine, warmth of home and abun-dance of memories.

Outside the windows pensive autumn spreads in the clear, gently warming light of the sun, the Nordic fall which I love as I do my very best friends be-cause it is so ripe and unconscious in its desireless-ness. The fruit drops from the tree without impact of the wind.

And so it is with the love of friends; without monition, without shaking, it drops down quietly and makes us happy. It wants nothing for itself and gives away everything.

Now compare the dreadfully greedy, sexual love with friendship!

I should think, further, that anyone who truly loves fall, few friends and loneliness may prognosti-cate for himself a great, fruitful and happy autumn of life.

53

"Thus suffer that of Parcae one
Spin me autumn, nice and long
From sunshine half congealed
And idleness."

But you know what idleness we mean,—did we not live together as *true* scholars, that is, loafers.

And what is hindering us to hope that life's autumn will bring us together again?

Let this be, thus, wish and hope, spoken on the memorable day of your birth, but enshrined in the heart always and forever!

From here I shall be visiting the old places of memory in Leipzig. Romundt has very congenially announced that he has already arrived there in order not to miss me. Did I write you that he has accepted my invitation to get the feel of being in Basel at the beginning of the winter semester and that there we shall solve the difficult problem of his future position together. Please write me your opinion. With my knowledge of him now after his nice unfolding in recent years, I regard him absolutely worthy of the prospect of a chair in philosophy. Understand well! Prospect! He will have much to do mastering systematically whole philosophical disciplines. Many a year may have to pass over it.

For the rest, I am longing for *our* meeting so much also because a whole lot of esthetic problems and answers have been bubbling within me for the last few years and the space of a letter is too small to be able to get something of it across to you. I am utilizing the occasion of *public* speeches in order to work out minor parts of the system, as I did, for instance, in my speech when I took up my duties at the university. Of course, Wagner is in a very pregnant sense beneficial especially as an example incomprehensible on the basis of traditional esthetics. The problem, above all, is to transcend vigorously Lessing's *Laokoon*, something one can hardly give voice to without being embarrassed and abashed inside.

Windisch has now taken up his teaching post at the university. The Brockhausens paid me a visit in Basel and we also were together for a day in Tribschen. Ritschl and his wife have quite an incredible love and esteem for me, a fact I am disclosing in order to gladden you. They really are extremely liberal people with a great deal of strength of their own. They permit whatever they differ with to exist cheerfully and without bias, thus doing honor to themselves.

I would be greatly surprised if they did not also judge you in this or a similar manner. All philologists should by now realize that we are good friends and quite different from all the others. Do you agree, dearest friend?

F. N.

I shall be here up to the 17th of October. The beautiful and useful collation of the *certamen* is a real service of friendship! My God, that such excellent friends like yourselves take upon themselves slaving over manuscripts and similar dreadful tasks for my sake!

(11) To Richard Wagner

Pater Seraphice, just as last year I was destined not to be an ocular witness to your birth celebration, so also this year an unfavorable constellation is preventing me from being present. Reluctantly the pen rushes into my hand even while entertaining hopes to be able to make a trip in May to your house.

Permit me to outline my birthday wishes within as narrow a compass and as personally as possible. Others may venture to offer you congratulations in the name of sacred art, in the name of the highest hopes for Germany, in terms of your own wishes. Let me be satisfied with the most subjective of all wishes: May you remain, as you have been this past year, my mystagogue for the secret doctrines of art and life. Should I, at times, appear to you somewhat distant beyond the gray mist of philology, personally I am not so distant. My thoughts are ever hovering around you. If it is true, as you have written—and I am proud of it—that I am guided by music, then you are at all events the orchestral leader in this my music. And it was you who told me that even something middling, if well conducted, can make a pleasing impression. In this spirit I express the strangest of all wishes: May it remain so, let the moment be stayed, it is so beautiful! Of the coming year I ask only that I may not prove myself unworthy of your inestimable sympathy and resolute encouragement. Please accept this wish along with the others you are receiving and with which you are starting this new year!

One of the "blessed boys."

(12) To Wilhelm Vischer(-Bilfinger)

Maderanertal, Monday, August 8, 1870

My dear Councillor:—Taking the present position of Germany into consideration, my decision to do my duty, as so many others have done, for our Fatherland may not come unexpectedly. With this in mind I am turning to you to ask you to grant me leave for the duration of the summer semester by interceding for me with the highly esteemed Council of Education. My state of health has improved to such an extent that, without hesitancy, I can make myself useful either as soldier or hospital attendant. That I am, indeed, *obligated* to cast my mite in the shape of my personal ability into the collection box of my Fatherland, no one will find so natural and worthy of approval as the Swiss Office of Education. Though I am quite aware of the extent of the obligations I must honor here at Basel, I could—in view of the tremendous call Germany has put out that everyone should do his duty as a German—allow myself to submit to their spell only under embarrassing pressure, which would not be of particular avail.

It came to my ear three weeks ago, provided I understood correctly, that Mr. Mähly would be able and glad to take over his classes again in the college. Perhaps Mr. Hagenbach or Mr. Gelzer could be prevailed upon in this unusual emergency to finish instructing the third class in Greek this summer. At any rate, I would ask these gentlemen personally to help me out, provided you will allow me to do so.

I shall return immediately to Basel in order to inform myself of the decision of the esteemed Office of Education and make a few preparations. Until then I would ask for your favor which, I hope, you will not withdraw in this case.

Respectfully,

Your most obedient Dr. Friedrich Nietzsche
Prof. o.p.

(13) To Erwin Rohde

Basel, Sunday, January (28), 1872

My dear and good Friend:—The other day I received a first enquiry through Susemihl whether I would accept a professorship at Greifswald but rejected it immediately and in your favor and recommending you. Are things progressing along that line? I have referred to Ribbeck.—The whole matter did become known here and awakened great sympathy for me among the good people of Baṣel. Although I protested saying it was not a call but only a quite preliminary enquiry, still the student body decided to hold a torchlight parade. Their motive was to give expression to how highly they have been regarding my activity in Basel thus far and hold me in esteem. By the way, I rejected the torchlight parade.

I am holding now lectures here "On the Future of Our Higher Educational Institutions" and have worked up to "something sensational" and even drawn enthusiasm here and there. Why can't we live together! For all that I have on my mind now and am preparing for the future cannot even be touched upon in letters.—I have made an alliance with Wagner. You cannot even imagine how close we are now and how our plans tie in.—What I have had to hear about my book is quite incredible, which is the reason why I am not writing anything about it.— What is your opinion? A tremendous sense of gravity overcomes me every time anything comes to my notice regarding it, because in these voices I divine the fate of what I am about to do. This life will become very difficult yet.

In Leipzig, they say, there is bitterness everywhere. Not a single word from anyone there, not even from Ritschl.—My good friend, at some time or other we must live together once again, it is a holy necessity. For some time past I have been living in a great stream. Almost every day brings me something amazing, and my aims and purposes likewise become elevated.—

Quite discreetly, and asking you to keep it secret, I am breaking the news to you that among other things I am preparing a *Promemoria* about the University of Strassburg as an interpellation of the Imperial Council, to be delivered to Bismarck. In it I intend to show how disgracefully one has let a tremendous moment slip by to found a truly German educational institution, to regenerate the German spirit and destroy the traditional so-called "culture." —War to the knife! or, to the cannons!

The Mounted Artillerist with the Heaviest Gun.

(14) To Hans von Bülow (*draft*)

(Basel, October 29, or shortly before, 1872)

Now, God be thanked that I have to hear this, and especially this, from you. I know full well how uncomfortable a moment I have given you. In answer I tell you how much good you have done me. Please give the following a thought. By and by I discarded every self-discipline while in musical training. I have never been given an opinion by any musician regarding my music. And I am truly happy to have been enlightened in such a simple way about the nature of my very last period during which I took up composing. For, unfortunately, I have to confess that I am making music of my own brand since childhood, gained my knowledge of theory by studying Albrechtberger, have composed fugues *en masse* and can achieve purity of style, that is, up to a degree of purity. Now and then, by contrast, I am overcome by such a barbaric, excessive urge, a mixture of spite and irony, that, like yourself, I can keenly sense what in the most recent modern music is meant to be serious, or is caricature and derision. I treated my fellow lodger (oh, the *boni!*) to it in the form of a pamphlet on programmatic music. The original characterization of the mood was *cannibalido*. Unfortunately, I am in all this quite clear in my mind that the whole, including the mixture of pathos and mischief, corresponded perfectly to a real mood and that I experienced more pleasure while bringing it down to paper than over any previous production. Thus, I am really in a bad way with my music and still more with my moods. How would you name a condition in which mirth, contempt, wantonness, sublimity got jumbled

60

up?—Here and there I lapse into this dangerous condition of being moonstruck.—Nevertheless, I am, you must know, far from judging and admiring Wagnerian music while in this state of psychiatric musical agitation. I know only one thing about my music and that is I become thus master over a mood which, if not catered to, is, perhaps, more harmful. In the case of Wagnerian music I just adore this highest necessity, and where I, as a poor musician, do not understand it, I presuppose it by an act of faith. But what amused me especially in the case of my last musical endeavors was just a certain caricature of that necessity while I was in a state of wildest exuberance. And it must have been exactly this desperate counterpoint which confused my feelings to a degree which drove me to absolute lack of judgment. In this extremity I occasionally held an even higher opinion of this type of music,—a greatly deplorable state from which you now have saved me. Please accept my thanks! It is, after all, not music? Then I am rather well off and need no longer bother at all with this kind of *otium cum odio*, with this rather odious way in which I have passed my time. I am concerned with truth. It is pleasanter to hear it than to tell it, as you well know. Thus, I am once more doubly in your debt.—Nevertheless, may I ask you one thing, not to make Tristan responsible for my sin? Such music as I wrote I would surely have been unable to compose *after* hearing Tristan,—he that cured me of my music for a long time. Would that I could hear him again!

Now then, I shall have to make an attempt at practicing musical hygiene. Perhaps I shall remain under your spiritual supervision and guidance if I study your edition of Beethoven's sonatas. For the rest all this is a very instructive experience for me. The *educational problem* which occupies my time in other fields is raised here in my own case with special vigor in the realm of art. To what frightful aberrations is this solitary person exposed now!

(15) To Richard Wagner

(Basel, middle of November 1872)

Beloved Master:—After all that has happened to me recently I truly have very little right to be in any manner whatever despondent. For I really live in the midst of a solar system of friendly love, comforting encouragement, and revivifying hopes. Still there is one point which disturbs me momentarily. Our winter semester has begun and I do not have any students whatsoever! Our students of philology have simply stayed away! It is really a *pudendum* and shamefacedly to be kept from all the world. I am telling you about it, beloved master, because you should know everything. The fact is, I have you know, it may be explained quite easily. Suddenly I have become of such ill repute among my colleagues that our little university bears the brunt! I am greatly tortured by all this, because I am actually very devoted and grateful to this university, and the last thing I would do is do it harm. But now my philological colleagues, including Councillor Vischer, are celebrating something they have never yet experienced in their entire academic careers. Up to the last semester the number of philologists was constantly on the increase, now it is suddenly as if they had all been blown away. Nevertheless, this is in agreement with what I hear from other university cities. Leipzig is, of course, blossoming forth again with envy and conceit. Everybody is condemning me and even those who "know me" cannot overcome their point of view which makes them commiserate me on account of this "absurdity." A professor of philology in Bonn whom I esteem greatly has dismissed his students simply with the statement that my book is "'pure nonsense" and one absolutely does not know what to do with it; somebody who writes like that is scientifically dead. In a similar vein I was told of a student who first wanted to come to Basel to study but then was held back in Bonn. He is now writing to a relative in Basel that he is thanking God for not having gone to a university where *I* am a teacher. Now would you believe that *Rohde's* noble undertaking will do anything else but increase doubly hatred and ill will and direct it against both of us? We both, Rohde and myself, fully expect this to happen and with absolute certainty. Still one could, at all events, bear that yet. But that I have done harm to a small university, a university which has placed a great deal of trust in me, hurts me much and may, in the long run, lead me to decisions which for other reasons have already come to my mind now and then.—For the rest, I can make good use of this winter semester, for as a simple schoolmaster I have to rely solely on the Pedagogical Institute.

This, indeed, was the "dark point." Apart from that all is light and hope. I would be a very morose mole were I not goaded to jump for joy upon receiving letters such as yours. It is true! You are coming! I praise my lucky stars and the dentist for this surprise I would never have even dared to dream.

Would you, perhaps, give "The Three Kings" a trial this time? I consider it better than Euler. This past summer I ate there with my sister and we passed a very delightful day with Miss von Meysenbug and the newlyweds Herzen-Monod.

Your magnificent piece about actors and singers again caused me to hope that someone will, at one time or another, write a comprehensive report on the basis of your esthetic researches and findings, the object being to show that within recent times the entire concept of art has so changed, become more profound and precise, that fundamentally nothing remains of traditional "esthetics." While on the Splügen Pass I reflected specifically on the choreographic determination of Greek tragedy, on the connection of sculpture with mimic art and the composition of the actors in groups. To come to the point, I can see how much Aeschylus himself furnished the *example* of what you write, so much so that even in our texts we should expect symmetries of motion in the wonderful numerical symmetries. Your tragedies inspire my earnest hope that beginning at this point, measure, limit, and rule must be found for a German style of movement, for a plastic reality. With these thoughts as an opening wedge my reading your dissertation struck me like a revelation.

Rohde's article has arrived. Don't you agree that when the pamphlet appeared I was right in maintaining that I was correct even in the most trifling points? It is always nice, however, to read proof of this by someone else. For, occasionally one becomes distrustful of oneself if the entire group of specialists speaks out so unanimously in hostile contradiction. But what did this poor friend have to suffer, having to spar for so long with such a "slave boy." If he suffered through it, it was the respect he owes you, beloved master, that gave him courage and strength. Now we two are happy to have *one* example, and how enviable I consider myself to have such a friend as Rohde. Am I not right?

Just as a curiosity I would like to relate to you that not so long ago I was consulted by a musician about an *operatic text*. The real reason behind it was that *I* should write it. I wrote him a sage letter and dissuaded him from the idea. As a counterproposal I told him he should compose a good *cantata* and try his hand once more on Goethe's *Walpurgisnacht, only do it better than Mendelssohn!* Will he do it?—The whole affair is really very droll.

May I express the hope that while you are sojourning in our beloved villainous Germany you keep with you the old and tried Bayreuth good luck. Please let me know very soon what preparations I should make for your stay here. With all my heart I say farewell to you now and, till we meet again!

Your old and loyal

F. N.

(16) To Paul Rée

Basel, October 22, 1875

Dear Doctor:—I had too much delight over your psychological observations than that I could take seriously your *A Dead Incognito (Posthumous Selections)*. While rummaging in a pile of new books I recently found your publication and immediately recognized some of the ideas as your property. Gersdorff had the same experience not so long ago when he quoted to me from former times: "To be able to be cozily silent together, they say, is, indeed, a greater indication of friendship than to be able to convivially talk together, as Rée maintains." You are, therefore, living on in me and my friends. And when I held your manuscript in my hands, which I esteem very highly, I regretted nothing more at that moment than to have been forced by a serious eye malady to leave off writing letters completely.

Far be it from me to presume praising you. Just as little do I wish to bother you with any "expectations" which I may entertain with regard to you. No! If you have nothing else printed ever than these maxims of *spiritual culture,* if this publication is and remains in fact your bequest, then all is well and good. Whoever lives and walks so independently has the right to be spared both praise and expectations. Nevertheless, in case you do intend to publish something again I would like to call your attention to the fact that you can always count with certainty on my publisher, E. Schmeitzner in Schloss-Chemnitz. I say this expressly because the only thing I cannot rejoice over when reading your book is the last page on which the writings of E. von Hartmann are gamboling one after the other. The book of a thinker, however, should not even on its posterior part give a reminder of the writings of a pseudothinker.

With all good wishes for your bodily weal and the request to kindly accept my gratitude for your having given your maxims at all to the public—for by it you demonstrate that the spiritual welfare of your fellow beings is your deep concern—I am

and remain

Yours,

Friedrich Nietzsche

(17) To Mathilde Trampedach

My dear Miss Trampedach:—You are going to write something for me today? Well, then, I too shall write something for you.—

Please gather all the courage your heart is capable of in order not to become frightened by the question I herewith put to you: will you become my wife? I love you and I feel as if you already belong to me. Not a word about the suddenness of my affection! At least there is no guilt involved and, hence, nothing needs be excused. But what I would like to know is whether you share the same feelings with me, that there was nothing strange at all between ourselves, not even for one moment! Don't you believe with me that in a union each of us will become freer and better than if we were single: *excelsior?* Would you dare walk with me as one who strives lustily for freedom and betterment and on all paths of life and thought?

Now, please, be frank and keep nothing back. Nobody knows about this letter and my enquiry except our mutual friend von Senger. At 11 o'clock tomorrow morning I shall return by express train to Basel. I have to return. I am enclosing my address in Basel. Should you be able to answer my question with a yes, I shall immediately write to your mother, in which case I would ask you for her address. Should you find it easy to decide quickly, be it yes or no, your decision would reach me by letter up to 10 o'clock at the *Hôtel garni de la Poste.*

Wishing you all good things and blessings forever.
Friedrich Nietzsche

(18) To Mathilde Trampedach

Basel, April 15, (1876)

My very dear Miss Trampedach:—You are so very generous to pardon me. I feel it by the gentleness of your letter, a gentleness I truly did not deserve. I suffered a great deal when I reflected on the cruel and violent way in which I behaved that I cannot be grateful enough to you for this indulgence. I do not want to offer any explanations and do not know how to justify myself. I have only one last wish, that if you should happen to read my name or should meet me again, please do not think of the fright which I have caused you. Under all circumstances I want you to believe that I would like to make good what evil I have committed.

    With esteem,

Yours

Friedrich Nietzsche

(19) To Erwin Rohde

(Basel, July 18, 1876)

Be it for good, dear, loyal friend, what you are announcing, be it truly for good! This I am wishing you from the bottom of my heart. I see, in this year of *grace*, 1876, you want to build your nest, like our Overbeck, and I hope I shall not lose you because you have thus become *happier*. Yes, I shall be able to think of you more calmly even though I should not follow you in this step. For you *needed* the *entirely trusty* soul so much, and have found *her* and hence *yourself* on a higher level. Things are different with *me*, heaven knows, or, perhaps, does not know. To me all this does not seem so necessary,—except on rare days.

It could be that there is a bad void in me. My desires and my needs are different. I hardly know how to say or explain it.

Tonight it occurred to me to put it into verse. I am not a poet, but you will probably understand me.

Through dark of night the wanderer strides
Briskly walking on.
The curvéd vale, extended hills—
Traversing all.
The night is beautiful—
He marches on and never rests,
Not knowing where the path will lead.
There, through the night, a bird is singing—
"Oh, bird, what art thou doing?
Why stayest thou my mind and foot
And pourest heart's sweet grief
Upon me, so I'm forced to halt
And hearken closely,
Interpreting thy voice and greeting?"
The good bird sings no more but says:
"No, wanderer, no! Not *you* I greet
With notes like these!
I sing because the night's so fair.
But *you* shall ever onward go
And never comprehend my song!
Just wander on;

69

And if your step sounds far away
I shall begin my song once more
As well I can.
So long, poor wandering man!"

So spoken to me, at night, after receiving your letter.
Also, the most cordial greetings of my sister.

F.N.

(20) To Louise Ott

Basel, August 30, 1876

My dear Mrs. Ott:—Darkness settled around me when
you left Bayreuth. It was as if someone had taken the
light from me. I first had to find myself once more.
That I did, and now you can take this letter to hand,
without apprehensions.

Let us hold fast to the purity of spirit which
brought us together. We shall remain loyal to each
other in all good things.

I think of you with such fraternal cordiality that
I could love your husband because he is *your* husband. Would you believe it, your little Marcel comes
to my mind ten times a day?

Would you like to receive from me my first three
Untimely Meditations? You ought to know what I
believe in, what I am living for.

Please keep me in good memory and help me in
what I consider my task.

With a pure heart,
I am Yours,
Friedrich Nietzsche

(21) To Louise Ott

Friday, Basel (September 22, 1876)

Dear, kind Friend:—First I *could* not write, then they made me undergo an eye treatment—and now I am not *permitted* to write for a long time to come! Nevertheless, I read your two letters again and again. I believe I read them too much, but this new friendship is like new wine, very pleasant, yet a little dangerous, perhaps?

For me at least it is.

But also for you when I realize what a freethinker you have fallen in with! A person who longs for nothing more than to get rid of some disquieting belief, who seeks and finds his happiness in this daily ever expanding liberation of the spirit. Could be that I even *want* to be more of a freethinker than I *could* be!

What to do next?—An *Elopement from the Seraglio* of belief, without Mozart's music?

Do you know the life history of Miss von Meysenbug with the title of *Mémoires d'une Idéaliste?*

What is the matter with poor little Marcel's teeth? We all must suffer before we can bite properly, physically and morally.—To chew in order to nourish ourselves is easily understood, of course; not to chew in order to chew!

Is there no good photograph of a certain beautiful, blond little lady?

Sunday a week I shall sojourn to Italy, to stay for a long while. From there you shall receive news. A letter addressed to me at Basel (Schützengraben 45) will reach me in any case.

With all my heart,

Fraternally yours,

Friedr. Nietzsche

(22) To Elisabeth Nietzsche

Sorrento, April 25, (1877)
Unstable weather all of the time

Nothing more cheerful than your letter, dearest sister,
which in every respect possible hit the nail on the
head. I was so badly off! Within a fortnight I was
six days in bed with six major attacks, the last absolutely desperate. When I got up Miss von Meysenbug
came down with rheumatism for three days. In the
depth of our misery we laughed a lot together when
I read her some selected passages from your letter.

Now, the plan which Miss v. M. regards as fixed
and to be kept in mind, and in whose execution you
must cooperate, is as follows. We are convinced that
I cannot in the long run continue at the University in
Basel, that I could do it only at the cost of all of my
more important projects and sacrificing at the same
time my health completely. Of course, winter next I will
still have to continue under the same circumstances,
but Easter 1878 there must be an end of it, provided
another combination is feasible, I mean marriage with
a compatible woman who must, however, be wealthy.
"Good, *but* rich," as Miss v. M. said, whereupon both
of us laughed heartily over the "but." With such a
one I would, then, spend the coming year at Rome,
which locality suits me equally for health, company
and studies. The project is to be promoted this summer in Switzerland so I would be able to return to
Basel in fall, married. A number of "beings" have
been invited to Switzerland, several with names un-
familiar to you, for instance, Elise Bülow of Berlin,
Elsbeth Brandes of Hanover. Respecting spiritual
qualities I always find Nat. Herzen best qualified.

72

You certainly did a great deal by idealizing the little Köckert in Geneva, praise, honor and glory be to you! Nevertheless, it is a delicate matter,—and where is the money?—

Rohde is to get the *Wagner* bust. Nothing further occurs to me; I excel in *stupidity*. Will you, therefore, be so good as to get this over with quickly by writing a brief letter to Rohde?

They have invited me to Frankfurt to give a talk on Wagner.—The translation of Mrs. Baumgartner's has *not* been approved by competent persons. This is confidential.

With traditional brotherliness,
Thine
Fritz, a Roman in the future
(provided I am alive another year)

As to the Bayreuth trouble you will be spared it, on which you are readily to be congratulated since the responsibility is too great. Lulu and the governess have taken full charge. Poor Loldi has been taken to an orthopedic institute in Altenburg.

(23) To Reinhart von Seydlitz

Basel, January 4, 1878

You are so good, dear, dear friend, in what you wish for me and hold out for the future. I am so poor at present. Each of your letters is a beautiful spark of joy in life, yet I cannot give you anything, in fact, nothing at all in return. Again, during Christmas recess, I spent bad, evil days, yes, weeks. Now we shall see what the new year *is able to produce*. Will it bring us together? I am holding this thought firmly in my mind.

Yesterday, Parsifal came to my home, sent by Wagner. First impression on reading it: There is more Liszt than Wagner, the spirit of the Counter-revolution. To me who am too much used to the Greek, the generally human, all this is too Christian, temporal, limited. It is all fanciful psychology. There is no flush, yet there is much too much blood—especially during Holy Communion everything seems to me too full blooded. Moreover, I do not care for hysterical women. Much that the inner eye can bear I will hardly be able to stand during the production. Just imagine our actors praying, trembling and their necks twisted in ecstasy. Even the interior of the Grail castle *cannot* be effective on the stage, just as little as the wounded swan. All these nice inventions belong in the epos and are meant, as I said, for the inner eye. What is spoken sounds as if it were a translation from a foreign tongue. Still, the scenes and how they follow one upon the other,—is that not highest poetry? Is that not the ultimate challenge to music?

So much for today. Please be satisfied with this. Truly devoted to you and your dear wife.

Your Friend

Nietzsche

P.S.—To judge by his letter addressed to me, Lipiner is a good pupil of Wagner. In passing, it would almost be desirable that he try and have Parsifal *poetized over* again.

(24) To Reinhart von Seydlitz

(Basel, June 11, 1878)

As far as I am concerned I always am glad and desirous that one of my friends do a good turn to Wagner and show him kindliness. For I am less and less capable of giving him joy, he being what he is, an *old*, unchanging man. His and my endeavors are widely apart. This hurts me sufficiently, but in the service of truth one must be prepared to bring any sacrifice. By the way, if he knew what designs I have in my heart *against* his art and his motives, he would think me one of his worst enemies which, as you know, I am not.

My last letter, was it *quite* obscure? In talking about the consequences of travelling the *via mala* I had reference to my views concerning morality and art (which are the toughest my sense of truthfulness has yet wrested from me!).

In a fortnight we shall have a general dissolution of our household. My dear sister is about to return forever to her mother.—Best thanks for the Hamde song; the translator, who is she?

Devoted to both of you from my heart

F. N. and L. N.

(25) To Mathilde Maier

My dear Miss Maier:—There is no other way, I have
to cause trouble to all my friends just by stating, at
last, whereby I myself get out of trouble. That meta-
physical mystification of all that is true and simple,
the struggle of reason *against* reason which tries to
see in all and everything either a marvel or an absurdity, and exactly corresponding to it a baroque art
with its exaggeration and glorified want of modera-
tion—I am referring to Wagner's art—all this contributed to making me, in the end, sick and sicker,
and threatened to almost rob me of my even temper
and ability. I wish you could also feel the pure *mountain air* in which I now am living my days. Coupled
with this I display a mellow mood toward those who
still live in the steamy valleys below. More than ever
I am determined and ready for all that is good and
sound, a hundred paces closer to the Greeks than
ever before. Would that you felt how I *myself* am
living, seeking wisdom in the minutest while before
I venerated the *wise* and adulated them. In brief, if
you are able to sympathize with me in this change
and crisis, I beseech you, you *must* want to experience something similar!

While spending the summer in Bayreuth I became
fully conscious of all this. After I attended the first
few performances I fled away to the mountains and
there, in a small woodland village I finished the first
sketch or about a third of my book, to which I had
then given the title "The Ploughshare." Following the
wishes of my sister I later returned to Bayreuth, having gained the inner composure to bear, in spite of

everything, the difficult-to-be-borne, and to bear it in *silence*, not speaking to anyone.—*Now* I am engaged in shaking off what does not belong to me, be it people, friend or foe, habits, conveniences, books. I shall live in solitude for years until, as a philosopher of *life*, fully matured and finished, *I allow myself* to (and then, perhaps, must) go again amongst men.

Would you, in the face of everything, remain as well disposed as you were toward me or, rather, could you remain so? You will perceive that I have arrived at a degree of honesty where I can tolerate human relations only in their absolutely pure state. Half friendships and the partisan spirit I avoid. Followers I do not want. May each man, or woman, be only *his, or her,* true disciple!

With cordial attachment and gratefully

F. N.

(26) To Malwida von Meysenbug

Naumburg, January 14, 1880

Although writing, for me, is forbidden fruit, you, whom I love and cherish like an older sister, shall nevertheless have a letter from me. It is probably going to be the last one! For the terrific and nearly incessant torture of my life makes me thirst for the end. There have been a few indications that the cerebral stroke which will release me is close enough on hand for me to entertain hopes. As far as agony and renunciation are concerned, I can compare my life in recent years with that of any ascetic of any period.

Nevertheless, I have gathered much during these years toward the purification and burnishing of the soul, and need neither religion nor art. (You will notice that I take pride in this. Indeed, being completely forlorn has permitted me for the first time to discover my own resources.) I believe I have accomplished my life's work, but like one to whom no time was left. Nevertheless, I know that I have poured out a drop of good oil for many and that I have given a large number of persons a hint of their own spiritual elevation, peaceableness and just sense. I am writing you this belatedly; really it should have been said when I completed my *Humanity*. No pain has been able and shall be able to lead me astray to become a false witness of life *as I see it*.

To whom could I say all this if not to you? I believe—though it is immodest to do so, don't you think so?—that our characters have many similarities. For instance, we both are courageous, and neither adversity nor disdain can divert us from the course which we have recognized as the right one. Then, too, both of us have experienced within and without many a thing whose radiance few of our contemporaries have beheld. We are full of *hope* for mankind and offer ourselves as modest sacrifices,—is that not your opinion also?—

Do you have good news from the Wagners? It is now three years that I have heard from them: *They*, too, have left me and I knew for some time past that from the moment that Wagner would notice the rift between our endeavors, he too would no longer be on my side. Someone told me that he is writing against me. Let him continue, the truth must come to light in one way or another! I think of him with lasting gratitude, for I owe to him some of the most powerful stimuli to spiritual independence. Mrs. Wagner, you know, of course, is the most sympathetic woman I have met in my life.—But, to reverse my attitude or even renew our contacts, for that I am totally unfit. It is too late.

To you my dear, sisterly and esteemed friend, the greetings of a youthful old man who does not bear a grudge toward life even though he must long for the end.

Friedrich Nietzsche

(27) To Elisabeth Nietzsche

Recoaro, June 19, 1881

Alas, my dear and good Sister, you think it is all about a *book?* Even you still take me as a writer?! My hour has come.—I would like to spare you *so much,* for you cannot carry my burden (it is ill fate enough to be such close kin to me). I would like you to be able to say to everyone with a clear conscience: "I am ignorant of my brother's more recent views." (No doubt they will let you know that they are "immoral" and "shameless.")—In the meantime, good cheer and courage, each for himself, and love, good and old!—

My address is General Delivery, St. Moritz in Graubünden (Switzerland). This is, once again, a *last* experiment. Since February I had to suffer extraordinarily, and only few locations are favorable.— Best thanks for your services regarding painter R.
Thine,

F.

(28) To Franz Overbeck

(Cancellation: Sils Engd.,
June 23, 1881)

I am greatly pleased, my dear Friend, that in this matter also our friendship remains steadfast, indeed, has *proven* itself anew. With forebodings I am thinking now and then of all the tests of fire and of cold to which persons dearest to me are being exposed by my "frankness." In the matter of Christianity you will probably believe me this one thing: In my heart I have never been vulgarly against it, and since childhood have taken much pains in all sincerity to understand its ideals. Ultimately, of course, the result was always that I found it absolutely impossible.—In this location, too, I have to suffer much. The summer, this time, is hotter and more saturated with electricity than ordinarily, which works to my disadvantage. This notwithstanding, I know of nothing more in tune with my nature than this spot in the upper reaches of the earth.—Mrs. Baumgartner has written me very nicely and cordially.—I do not yet have my own book.—Hellwald has been gratefully received. It is a compendium of a group of opinions.

With cordial feelings of devotion to you and your wife

F. N.

I positively know no longer with what views I am pleasing people and with which I am causing injury.

(29) To Franziska Nietzsche

Sils-Maria, middle of July, 1881

My dear Mother:—I am very sorry over your and our loss! Our Theobald was such a gentle and good person, severe with himself and yet not fanatic. We shall always be deeply touched when remembering him.

Now, only one word about myself so as to bring comfort to your minds. I reproach myself for my stupidity in having written you only brief notes concerning my health and nothing more. In this way you must have received a wrong impression about myself. There never was a man to whom the expression "depressed" applied less. Those who can discern a little more of my purpose in life and how it must be unceasingly promoted are of the opinion that I am, if not the *happiest*, at least the most daring of men. More weighty things rest upon me than mere considerations of health, and I shall manage to square myself with them also. My appearance, by the way, is excellent, my musculature is almost like that of a soldier because I am taking prolonged walks. Everything is in order with my stomach and abdomen. My nervous system is splendid in view of the immense work it has to do; it is quite sensitive but very strong, a source of astonishment to me. Even the long and severe maladies, an occupation which did not suit me, and a dead wrong treatment have not harmed it basically. Indeed, within the past year it has become stronger and owing to it I have produced one of the most daring, the sublimest and deepest of books ever spawned by human brain and heart. Even had I committed suicide in Recoaro, a man would have died

81

who was the most indomitable, and absolutely superior, not one who had given up in despair. With respect to the scientific material I require, I am in a better position than any and all physicians. More yet, my scientific pride is offended when you are suggesting that I should submit to new treatments and even express the opinion that I "did not do anything for my sickness." You should have a little more confidence in me in these matters! Up to now I have been under my own governance for only two years, and if I did make any mistakes it was always owing to the fact that I ultimately yielded to the earnest entreatments of others and submitted to experimentation. Into this category belong my stay in Naumburg, in Marienbad, etc. Moreover, every competent physician has prognosticated my recovery but not before *a number of years* have elapsed. Above all, I must try and get rid of the grave aftereffects of all those wrong methods by which I have been treated for such a long time. I implore you, don't be angry with me if I seem to reject your love and sympathy in this matter. I fully intend to continue henceforth as my own physician. Moreover, people shall say after I am dead that I was a *good* physician,—and not only in my behalf.—Be that as it may, I shall still have to look forward to many, many periods of illness. Do not become impatient the while, I beg of you with all my heart! This makes me more irritable than the sickness itself, because it demonstrates to me that my nearest relatives display so little faith in me.

Whoever could secretly look on me as I am practicing combining concern for my own recovery with promoting my great tasks, would pay me no mean compliment. Not only do I live courageously, but reasonably to the highest degree, supported by my ex-

tensive medical knowledge and continuous observation and research.

With all my heart and praying that you may not
take anything badly,

Your Son and Brother

Please write about *good* things to me at this height
where I am brooding over the future of mankind. Let
us leave all the little, personal sufferings and cares by
the wayside.

(30) To Franz Overbeck

(Cancellation: Sils-Engd., July 30, 1881)

I am absolutely astonished and quite enraptured!
I have a *precursor*, and what a herald he is! I was
practically ignorant of Spinoza. That I am *now* hankering after him was the result of "instinct." Not only
is his over-all objective like mine—to raise knowledge
to the *mightiest* effect—but, in five of the main points
of his doctrine I find myself. The most abnormal and
the lonesomest of thinkers is closest to me especially
in *these* things: He denies freedom of will, purposes,
a moral world order, whatever is nonegoistic, and
evil. Of course, the differences also are tremendous,
but they lie more in the difference of age, culture,
and science. *In summa:* My solitude which, as on
very high mountains, often, very often caused me to
be short of breath and the oozing of blood, has at
least for the time being become the isolation of two.
—Strange!

By the way, my health is not as expected. Exceptional weather here also! Eternally changing atmospheric conditions—this will drive me yet from Europe! I must have *clear skies for months* at a stretch, otherwise I do not make progress. Already six heavy attacks lasting two to three days!—

Cordially

Your

Friend

(31) To Paul Rée

(Genoa, March 21, 1882)

My dear Friend: What pleasure do your letters bring me!—They draw me off to all sides and ultimately by all means to you!—Yesterday, on the Mediterranean, exactly on that famous spot where . . . just imagine . . . had such a surprise attack while bathing, and because . . . I laughed heartily over your 30 francs.— The post office handed me this letter without even asking for my passport, and the young officer sends his greetings to you—*ecco!*—Overbeck sent me my money.—Now I am provided for for a couple of months.—Please send my greetings to this young Russian lady, if it makes sense at all. I am hankering after that type of soul. Better still, I shall soon go on rapine for it. In view of what I intend to do in the next ten years I need her! Marriage is something else again—I could consent to getting married at the most for two years, and this also only in view of what I have to do in the next ten years.—After the experiences which I just had with Köselitz, we shall never

84

bring him around to accept money from us, be it in the most bourgeois fashion of buying and selling. Yesterday I wrote him whether he would sell me and two other friends the *Matrimonio* score. I offered him 6000 francs, payable in four yearly installments of 1500 francs. This proposal I consider elegant and a snare. As soon as he agrees I shall let you know and you will be so good as to make a deal with Gersdorff.

So long! The typewriter refuses to function, it is the spot where the ribbon was mended.

I wrote to Miss von Meysenbug, also in regard to Pierre's.

Heartiest wishes for your well-being, be it by day or by night.

Your loyal friend

F. N.

I am sending the letter for Miss von M. to General Delivery, Rome, because I do not have her address.

No, I am going to send the letter to Miss von M. to *your* address, dear friend!

(32) To Lou von Salomé

(Naumburg, supposedly June 10, 1882)

Now, my dear Friend, from where I am I do not see at all which persons are to be *necessarily* initiated into our intentions. But I should think that we ought to keep to our plan of *initiating* only indispensable persons. I like living in seclusion and desire with all my heart that a European gossip may be spared both you and me. For the rest, I have such high hopes for our living together that all unavoidable and accidental side-effects impress me but little for the moment. Moreover, *whatever* troubles should arise, we shall bear them *together* and *together* we shall throw each evening the entire little pack into the water, what do you say?

What you tell me about Miss v. Meysenbug will cause me to write her a letter soon.

May I know how you intend to pass the time after Bayreuth and to what extent you are counting on me? Presently I need mountain air and timber forest badly. Not only health, but still more *The Gay Science* drive me into solitude. I want to put an *end* to it.

Would it be convenient if I should come to Salzburg (or Berchtesgaden) right away, that is, on my way to *Vienna?*

When we are together I shall write you something in the book you sent.—

Finally. I am inexperienced and untrained in all things requiring action. For years I *never had to* explain or justify any of my activities to anybody. My plans I prefer to keep under cover, what I have *done* let all the world talk about!—Nevertheless, nature has provided every being with different weapons of defense. To you she has given the magnificent candor of will power. Pindar once said: *"Become* what you *are!"*

Loyally and devotedly

F. N.

(33) To Lou von Salomé

(Tautenburg, July 2, 1882)

My dear Friend:—Now the heavens above are bright! Yesterday noon everything happened around me as if I were celebrating my birthday. *You* sent me word about your consent, the most beautiful present anyone could have made me at this time. My sister sent me cherries. Teubner sent me the first three printed sheets of *The Gay Science*. To top it all, the very last part of the manuscript had just been finished and with it the work of six years (1876-1882), the period of my entire "freethinking!" Oh, what years! What tortures of all sorts, what feelings of loneliness and weariness unto death! And against all this, as it were, against death *as well as life,* I have concocted this my medicine, these my thoughts with their little strip of *cloudless sky* above. Oh, dear friend as often as I think of all this emotion stirs within me and I am deeply touched, unable to account for the achievement of success. Self-pity and a triumphant feeling fill my whole being. For it is a victory, a complete one at that, inasmuch as even bodily health has reappeared, I know not wherefrom, and everyone tells me that I look younger than ever. Heaven preserve me from follies! But from now on when *you* will be my guide, I shall be *well* advised and need not be afraid.—

Concerning the coming winter I have thought *seriously and exclusively* of Vienna. My sister's plans for the winter are quite independent of mine, *no* ulterior motives are involved. The South of Europe is now no longer on my mind. I do not want to be lonely any longer and desire to learn how to become human. Oh! for *this* lesson I have to learn almost everything yet!—

Please accept my thanks, dear friend! *Everything* will be alright just as you said.

Most cordial greeting to our Rée.

Entirely *Yours,*

F. N.

(34) To Elisabeth Nietzsche

Naumburg, beginning September 1882

In two or three days, my dear Lisbeth, I am off. I wrote to Eisers whom I want to visit in Frankfurt, and as soon as I get Sulger's address from you everything will be in order. On yesterday I received two postals from *you*—from Messina, by way of Rome and Basel. All due respects to the postal system!—

The work I planned for Naumburg, a composition, I have also accomplished very nicely and thus satisfied myself.

If I could only convey to you the conviction of joyous confidence in the future which animated me this summer. I have succeeded in *everything* and in some things against expectations and at the very instant I thought I would fail. Lou also is quite satisfied (she is entirely swamped with work and buried in books). What concerns me most intimately is that she has converted Rée, as he himself writes, to one of my main views which will change the *very foundation* for his book. Rée wrote yesterday that "Lou has, without question, grown a few inches in Tautenburg."

I note with sadness that you still have to suffer from the aftereffects of those scenes which I would most gladly have spared you. However, keep in mind only that in the excitement of these scenes there came *to light* what might otherwise have remained in the dark for a long time, that is, that Lou had a *meaner* opinion of myself and *some lack of confidence* in me, and when I weigh more accurately the circumstances of our having become acquainted, she was probably quite entitled to it, not to forget the effects of some careless remarks by our friend R. Nevertheless, she now has a *better* opinion of me, and is *that* not the main thing, my dear sister? For the rest if I think of the future it would be hard on me were I to assume that you did not share my feelings regarding Lou. We have such an identity of gifts and motives that sometime or other our names are bound to be mentioned together, and every disparagement to which she may be subject will hit me first.

However, I may have said *too much* about this point. Once more I thank you from the bottom of my heart for all the goodness you have shown me this summer, and I truly and deeply appreciate your sisterly feelings even at times when you were not able to feel as I did. Indeed, who could have anything to do with me, an antimoral philosopher, without running into danger! Two things my mode of thought absolutely forbids me, first, regret, secondly, moral indignation.—

Think kindly of me again, dear Llama!

Thine Brother

(35) To Louise Ott

(Naumburg on the Saale River,
September 1882)

Esteemed Friend, or may I, after six years, no longer use *this* word?

In the meantime I have lived closer to death than to life and have, consequently, become a little too much of a "sage" and nearly a "saint." . . .

Be that as it may, *that* could perhaps still be corrected! For once again I believe in life, in people, in Paris, even in myself—and want to see *you* again and not too long hence. My last book is entitled *The Gay Science.*

Is the sky bright much of the time in Paris? Do you know by chance of a room which may be suitable for me? It would have to be a very simple room, dead quiet, and not too far away from you, my dear Mrs. Ott.

Or do you advise against coming to Paris? Perhaps it is not a place for hermits, for people who would like to carry their life's task about with them and care not two straws for politics and the contemporary world?

The memory of you is so lovely!

Cordially yours,

Professor Dr. F. Nietzsche

(36) To Franz Overbeck

Address: Auenstrasse 26, 3rd floor,
Leipzig (September 1882)

My dear Friend:—Once again I am sitting in Leipzig, the old city of books, in order to become acquainted with a few volumes before I am off again. Probably nothing will come of the German winter campaign, I need clear weather in every respect. Yes, *character* this cloudy sky over Germany has, and, I reckon, the music of Parsifal possesses likewise character, but a *poor* one. Lying before me is the first act of *Matrimonio Segreto*,—golden, glittering, good, *very good* music.

The weeks in Tautenburg did me good, especially the last ones. By and large I can rightfully speak of recovery even though I am frequently reminded of the *unstable equilibrium* of my health. But, let the sky above me be *clear,* or I lose too much in time and vigor!

If you have read the *Sanctus Januarius* you will have noticed that I have passed through one *tropic*. All that lies before me is new and it won't be long before I shall get to see the *terrible* sight of my future task in life. This long, rich summer was a period of *probation* for me. I took leave of it extremely courageously and with pride, for I felt that at least during this span of time the otherwise so hateful gap between willing and accomplishing was *bridged*. *Severe* demands were made on my humanity and I have done all right even in most difficult situations. This entire intermediate condition between other times and at one time I call *in media vita*. The demon of music which visited me again after long years has compelled me to speak of it in sound also.

The most useful occupation this summer, however, were my talks with Lou. Our intelligence and our tastes are of one kin deep down. But apart from that the contrasts are so many that we constitute mutually the most instructive objects and subjects of instruction. I have not come to know anyone till now who knows how to distil from his experiences such an amount of *objective insights,* not anyone who is capable of extracting so much from all he has learned. Yesterday Rée wrote me, "Lou has decidedly grown a few inches while in Tautenburg." Well, perhaps I too have grown. I would like to know whether such a *philosophic frankness* as exists between us has ever existed before. L. is now totally engrossed in books and work. The greatest service she has done me thus far is to have persuaded Rée to recast his book on the basis of my main thoughts. I fear her health will hold out only six or seven years.

Tautenburg gave Lou an *objective.*—She left behind her a stirring poem "Prayer to Life."

Unhappily my sister has developed into a deadly enemy of L's. She was full of moral indignation from beginning to end and now maintains she knows what is the matter with my philosophy. She wrote to my mother, "at Tautenburg she saw my philosophy come alive and was terrified: *I* love evil while *she* loves the good. If she were a good Catholic she would enter a convent and atone for all the harm that will come of it." In brief, I have the Naumburg "virtue" against me. There is really a *break* between us, and my mother also forgot herself once in a word to such an extent that I had my trunks packed and left early in the morning for Leipzig. My sister (who did not want to come to Naumburg so long as I was there and is still in Tautenburg) quoted *à propos* ironically: "Thus began Zarathustra's decline."—Indeed, it is the *beginning* of the *beginning*.—This letter is for you and your dear wife. Do not think of me as an enemy of men.

Most cordially
Thine
F.N.

The heartiest greetings to Mrs. Rothpletz and yours! I also wish to thank you for your cordial letter.

(37) To Gottfried Keller

Auenstrasse 26, Leipzig, September 1882

Highly Revered Sir:—I wish you already knew through someone that you are just this for me, a very highly revered person, man and poet. For then I would not have to ask your pardon today for having sent you a book some time back.

Perhaps this book will hurt you despite its cheerful title? Now, by all that is true, whom would I like to hurt less than yourself who causes gladness to enter every heart! My thoughts of you are so full of gratitude!

Cordially yours,
Dr. Friedrich Nietzsche

(38) To Heinrich von Stein

(S. Margherita)
Beginning December 1882

But, my dear Doctor, you could not have answered me more beautifully than you did, sending me your sheets! It was a coincidence! Now in all first encounters such a good "augury" should be present.

You are, assuredly, a poet! I have the feeling that the passions, their change, but not least the scenic apparatus, are effective and *credible* (all, indeed, depends on this!).

In the matter of linguistic expression—well, let us talk about language when we meet; this is no proper subject to be discussed in a letter. It seems certain, dear Doctor, that you are still *reading* too many books, especially German books! How is it possible to read a German book!

Oh, I beg your pardon! I did it myself just now and shed tears the while.

Wagner, at one time, said of me that I was writing Latin, not German. For one it is true and then again it sounds well to my ears. In all that is German I just can partake only of a part, no more. Consider my name. My ancestors were Polish nobles, even the mother of my grandfather was a Pole. Now, I make a virtue of my being half German and claim to know more about the *art* of the language than it is possible for *Germans* to do.

With reference to this discussion, more when we meet.

As to the "hero" I do not entertain such a high opinion of him as you. At any rate, he represents the type of human existence which is most acceptable, especially when there is no other choice.

One takes a liking to something, and hardly has one conceived a fundamental love for it when the tyrant in us (whom we are altogether too ready to call "our higher self") urges us: "Give me *that* as a sacrifice." And we bring it as a sacrifice; yet there is animal torture and roasting over slow fires. What you are treating of are, practically, all problems of cruelty. Are you enjoying that? I tell you in all frankness that I myself have too much of this "tragic" complex in my body as not to *curse* it on occasion. My experiences, in small things and in large ones, always take the same course. It is then that I long most for an *eminence* from which I can see the tragic problem spread out below me.—I would like to *take away* from human existence something of its heart-breaking and cruel character. However, to be able to go on with this theme, I would have to let you in on a secret which I have not yet divulged to anyone, that is, the task with which I am confronted, my life's work. No, of this we ought not to converse. Or, rather, the two of us being what we are, two separate natures, ought not even *keep silent about* it together.

Deeply grateful and with regards,

F. Nietzsche

I am again residing in Genoa or vicinity, more hermit than ever: General Delivery, Santa Margherita Ligure (Italy).

(39) To Lou von Salomé and Paul Rée

(Fragment. Middle of December 1882)

My dear Lou and Rée:—Please do not be too much disturbed about the eruptions of my "megalomania" or my "injured vanity." And even if I should, by chance, yielding to some impulse or other, take my life there would not be too much to be sad over. What concern have you with my whimsical ideas! (Even my "truths" have not concerned you till now.) Both of you please get together and ponder on this very carefully that, in the last analysis, I am touched in the head, half ready to be confined to the lunatic asylum, totally confused by my long loneliness.

I have arrived at what I call *reasonable* insight into how things stand after I took a tremendous dose of opium, out of despair. But instead of losing my mind, I seem to have at last *come to* my mind. By the way, I was sick for weeks, and if I say that for 20 days we had Orta weather here, I need say no *more*.

Friend Rée, please ask Lou to forgive me everything; she too is giving me an occasion to forgive her. Up to now I have not forgiven her.

It is more difficult to pardon your friends than it is to pardon your enemies.

There with Lou's defense . . .

(40) to Franz Overbeck

(Cancellation: Rapallo,
December 25, 1882)

Dear Friend:—Perhaps you never received my last letter?—This last *morsel of life* was the hardest I have chewed thus far and it is still possible I will *choke* on it. I have suffered from the insulting and agonizing experiences of this summer as if I had been insane—the hints I gave you in Basel and in my last letter always kept the most essential things under cover. There is a cleavage of opposite impulses which I cannot cope with. That is to say, I flex all fibers of my self-control, but I have lived too long in solitude and off my own substance, as it were, that I am now being broken on the wheel of my own passions more than anyone else. If I could only sleep! But the strongest dosages of my soporifics help me just as little as my walking six to eight hours.

If I do not succeed in the alchemist's trick to make gold even of this muck, then I am lost.—I have the *most beautiful* occasion to prove that, to me, "all experiences are useful, all days are holy and all men are divine!!!"

All men divine.—

My suspicion is at present very extensive. In everything that comes to my ears I feel there is a hidden contempt. For instance, even in a recent letter of Rohde's. I could swear that he now would sit in judgment over me and my aims in the most despicable manner if, by chance, there had not been earlier relations of friendship between us.

Yesterday I also stopped writing letters to my mother. I could not bear it any longer and it would have been better had I refused to bear it earlier. *In how far* the inimical judgments of my relatives have spread in the meantime and given me a bad name,—well, I would rather know it than suffer from the uncertainty.

My relationship with Lou is breathing its most painful last. So at least I believe today. Later if there is a later, I shall say something about it. *Pity*, my dear friend, is a sort of hell, no matter what the disciples of Schopenhauer may say.

I am not asking you "what shall I do?" A few times I thought of renting a little room in Basel, visiting you now and then, and listening to lectures at the university. Sometimes I thought of the opposite, to reduce my solitude and resignation to the ultimate and—

Well, let this be as it may! Dear Friend, you and your revered and intelligent wife,—you are nearly the last strip of safe ground I have. Odd!

May all be well with you.

Your

F. N.

(41) To Paul Deussen

(Genoa, March 16, 1883)

That is nice, dear old friend! That is the way to do it, unfold each of one's seven powers, gather them up at last and then make toward the goal with seven horses. Much had to meet in one person in order for him to be able to reveal such a doctrine as that of the Vedānta to us Europeans. And not the least I sing your praises, old friend of mine, in that you have not forgotten how to work vigorously. Was not Μελέτη the name of one of the three Muses? Heaven knows, without honest diligence only weeds grow in the most beautiful garden plot. Seen at short range even the best of artists should not distinguish himself from the craftsman. I hate those scoundrels who do not care for craftsmanship and treat the life of the spirit only as an epicurean venture.

I am thoroughly glad to make the acquaintance for once with the classical expression of a mode of thinking totally foreign to me. Your book has done that for me. In it everything I suspected in view of this mode of thinking comes out into the open most naïvely. Page after page I am reading completely "wantonly."—You could not wish for a more *grateful* reader, dear friend!

By chance they are typesetting at this very moment my *Manifesto* which with just about the same eloquence says yea. where your book says nay. One could laugh over this. Perhaps it will hurt you and I am not sure in my mind whether I should send the book to you. In order to be able to write your book you *could not* think as I do, and your book *had to* be written. Consequently—

Thanking you from my heart

Friedrich Nietzsche

(42) To Malwida von Meysenbug

(Genoa, end of March 1883)

My dear Friend, in the meantime I have taken the decisive step and all is in order. To give you an idea of what it is all about I enclose the letter of my *first* "reader," my excellent Venetian friend who also is my helper now that I am going to press.—

I shall leave Genoa as soon as I can and am going into the mountains. *This* year I want to meet no one.

Do you care to have a new name for myself? The language of the church *has* one: I am . . . the *antiChrist*.

Please do me the goodness and do not forget how to laugh!

Entirely Yours, devotedly

F. Nietzsche

Salita della Battistine 8 (*interno* 4), *Genoa*.

(43) To Malwida von Meysenbug

Genoa, beginning April 1883

Don't you want to laugh a little with me, my very dear friend? I am enclosing a card from the author of that letter.—Take into due consideration that we are living toward the end of the nineteenth century! And the writer is apparently an intelligent person, a sceptic—just ask my sister!

It is a most wonderful story: I have challenged all religions and produced a new "holy book!" And

100

in all seriousness it is as serious as any even though it incorporates laughter into religion.—

How is your health? End of winter I was badly off. A violent *fever* tortured me for nearly five weeks and tied me to the bed. How fitting that I should live alone!

Can I be sure that you will save the two curiosities or return them to me on occasion? Up to the 25th I (what I am *very much* so in essence) shall be in Genoa still.

Esteeming you with all my heart,

Nietzsche

The remark in the middle of the card is *good.*—Indeed I have "committed" the feat (and the stupidity) of writing the *commentaries* sooner than the text.— But, pray, *who* has *read* them? I mean, studied them for years? A single one, so far as I know, and *because of that* he now enjoys the text too.

Last year in Germany I found the superficiality of judgment matured to the point of imbecility in that they confused me with Rée!!! Now, *you* know *what* is the meaning of that—!!!

(44) To Malwida von Meysenbug

Sils-Maria, Engadin (Switzerland), August 1883

My dear, highly esteemed Friend,—or is it immodest if I call you that? It is certain that I have excessive good faith in you and, hence, it does not matter very much what words I use.

I have had a *bad* summer and am still having it.

Last year's bad deal descended once more upon me and I had to listen to so *much* that spoiled the magnificent solitude of nature and nearly converted it into hell. After all that I have heard *of late*, oh! much too late! these two persons, Rée and Lou, are not worth licking *my boots*.—Pardon this all-too male simile. It is a long drawn-out misfortune that this R., a liar and sneaky slanderer at heart has crossed my path. And just look, the great patience and pity I have had so far as he is concerned! "It is a poor fellow, one has to egg him on"—how often did I not say that when his miserable and insincere manner of thinking and living nauseated me! I shall not forget the rage which I felt in 1876, but kept under control, when I heard that he would come and visit you at Sorrento. Two years ago the same concealed anger flared up in me. I was here in Sils-Maria and became *ill* at the news received from my sister that he wanted to come up here. One should place more trust in one's instincts, even the instincts of *resistance*. But, Schopenhauer's "pity" has always and up to now played the *main mischief* in my life. Therefore I have every reason to favor *such* moral systems as will count yet a few other motives among morality and not attempt to reduce our entire human vigor to "sympathetic feelings." This is not only a weakness at which every magnanimous Greek would have laughed, but it is a serious practical danger. One should make *his* ideal of *mankind prevail*, one should discipline and overpower his fellow beings as well as himself with his ideals, and thus act creatively! To do *that*, however, means bridling one's sympathy pretty much and treating as *inimical* whatever goes *counter* to our ideals (as, for example, scoundrels such as L. and R.).—You are listening in *while* I am giving *myself* a "lesson in morality." But it nearly cost me my life to penetrate to this "wisdom."—

I should have spent the summer with you and in the noble circle surrounding you; but now it is too late!

Yours with all my heart and gratefully

Nietzsche

(45) To Franz Overbeck

(From Sils-Maria, received August 28, 1883)

(This letter is for you alone)

Dear Friend:—Being separated from you threw me back into the darkest melancholy, and during the entire trip back I could not rid myself of evil, black sensations. Amongst them was a veritable hatred of my sister who, for a whole year now, by being silent at the wrong time and talking at the wrong time has caused me to fail in superbly overcoming myself, so as to become in the end the victim of a merciless feeling of revenge just at the moment when, in my inmost thinking, I had renounced all revenging and punishing. This inner conflict brings me step by step closer to insanity.* I feel this most menacingly, and I do not know to what extent a trip to Naumburg could lessen this danger. *Quite on the contrary*, dreadful scenes might occur momentarily, and this long-fanned hatred could come to the fore in words and deeds, in which case *I* would, by far, be more

*Could you, of all people, perhaps get this point energetically across to my sister?

victimized than anyone else. Even writing letters to my sister is now hardly advisable, except such letters as are entirely harmless (even recently I sent her a letter full of cheerful verses). It could be that my reconciliation with her was the most tragic step in this whole mess. *Now* I can see clearly that she believes she is *thus* entitled to her revenge against Miss Salomé.—Excuse me!

After having agreed on the delicate situation involved in the Leipzig plan it was truly good to find a letter from Heinz with which this whole matter has been brought to a close. It was done in desperation on my part. I enclose his letter, together with the first public utterance regarding *Zarathustra I.* Oddly enough it was penned in a jail. What pleases me is to see that even this first reader gets the feeling of what it is all about, that is, the long promised "anti-Christ." Not since Voltaire has there been such a *murderous attempt* against Christianity and, to tell the truth, even Voltaire never had an inkling that one could attack it in *this* way.—

As concerns *Zarathustra II,* Köselitz writes: "Z. has a tremendously powerful effect. It would, however, be rash to attempt to express an opinion about it at this time. It knocked me down, I am still lying on the floor."—

You understand!

At the time of my visiting with you my old school chum Krug wanted to call on me. (He is Director of the Royal Rail Road Traffic Office in Köln, it says on his visiting card.)

Köselitz's letter has some statements about *Epicurus* (as once before he had written about *Seneca*) which I canot compare with anything else so far as

104

factual knowledge of *this type* of philosophy and insight into human character are concerned. He hints he has some "philologists in ordinary" whom he is goading on to go to the library to study the church fathers and other scribblers with *Epicurus* in mind.

How good it was to have you and your heartfelt confidence for once so close to me! And how well we understand and understood each other! May your reason, more securely anchored, be and remain a support for my reeling head!

Cordially your friend

Nietzsche

(46) To Erwin Rohde   (Nice, Februry 22, 1884)

My dear old friend, I do not know how it happened, but when I read your last letter and especially when I saw the lovely picture of the child, it was as if you were pressing my hand, looking at me dejectedly, melancholically, as if to say: "How is it possible at all that we still have so little in common and live, as it were, in different worlds? And at one time—"

And so, my friend, it is with all people who are dear to me. All is *over and done with,* all is past history, indulgence. One still meets, one speaks in order not to be mute, one writes letters in order not to be silent. Truth, however, expresses itself in the glance. And that tells me (I hear it quite well!): "Friend Nietzsche, you are not *completely* alone!"

This is the way things have turned out for me at last.

Meanwhile, I continue on my way. In reality it is a journey, an ocean journey. It is not for nothing that I lived for years in the city of Columbus.—

My *Zarathustra* has been finished in three acts. The first one you have, the two others I hope I will be able to send you in four to six weeks. It is a sort of abyss of the future; something gruesome there is especially in his beatitude. All that you find in it is my own, without prototype, comparison, precursor. Whoever has once *lived* in it returns into this world, his countenance changed.

Of this, however, one should not speak. For your benefit as a *homo litteratus*, I will not hold back with a confession. I fancy that with this Z. I have brought the German language to perfection. After *Luther* and Goethe a third step had to be taken. Look and see, my old bosom comrade, whether or not strength, suppleness and euphony have ever been found together in our language as they are here. Read Goethe after a page of my book and you will find that the quality of "undulating" which is Goethe's as a draftsman, also is not foreign to the language creator. I am superior to him in the more severe, masculine line without, however, winding up with Luther among the uncouth. My style is a *dance*, a play of symmetries of various kinds and a leaping over and mocking of these symmetries. This extends right into the choice of vowels.—

Forgive me! I should guard against making such a confession to anyone else, but you expressed once —as the only one, I believe—pleasure in my language.

For the rest, I have remained a *poet* to the limit of the concept, even though I have *tyrannized* myself thoroughly with the opposite of all poetizing.

Oh, my friend, what a frantic reticent life I am living! So alone, so very much alone! So without "children!"

Please keep me in your good graces. Truly, my good thoughts are always with you.

Thine

F. N.

(47) To Franz Overbeck

San Canciano calle nuova 5256,
Venice (received May 2, 1884)

My dear Friend Overbeck:—After all is said and done it is very nice that in the years just past we have not become alienated, not even by Zarathustra, it would seem. I never had illusions about the possibility of my being *very* lonely as I am approaching my 40th year. I also know that *much* evil is still going to come *my way*. Not too long hence they will teach me *how dearly* one has to pay for "reaching for the highest crown," to use the stupid and false language of the *ambitiosi*.

Meanwhile, I want to utilize well and put to advantage the position I have captured. It is highly probable that I am at present *the most independent man in Europe*. My aims and tasks are much more voluminous than those of anyone else. What I call grand politics at least furnishes a *good* station and provides a bird's eye view of present-day events.

Concerning all practical aspects of life, I beg you,

loyal and tried friend, to keep on guarding *one* thing so far as I am concerned, I mean this greatest possible independence and freedom from *personal* considerations. I believe you can appreciate what Zarathustra's admonition "Become hard!" has to say especially to me. My disposition to have justice prevail against everyone, as well as to treat especially what is basically most inimical to me, with the greatest leniency is developed in me excessively and harbors dangers upon dangers not only for me but for my undertaking. For that I need steeling myself and, for the sake of discipline, I must be occasionally cruel.

I beg your pardon! It does not always sound well if one talks of oneself, neither does it always smell sweetly.

As to my health, it seems I am over the hump. The winters I shall pass in Nice. In summer I need a city with a large library where I can live *incognito*. (I thought of Stuttgart, what is your opinion?)

I am still thinking of living this year again in Sils-Maria where my book basket is stored, provided I know how to protect myself better against the importunities of my sister than I did last year. She really has become a very vicious person. A letter full of the most poisonous insinuations against my character, which I received from her in January and which is a nice companion to the letter she wrote Mrs. Rée, has now made me see things sufficiently clearly: —*she must go away to Paraguay.* I myself wish to break off all intercourse with those who take my sister's part. From now on I cannot stomach any "half-and-half" attitude against me any longer.

Here I am, in Köselitz's home, in the quietude of

Venice and am listening to music which in itself is often a kind of ideal Venice. Let me tell you, he is progressing toward a more *masculine* art; the *new* overture of the *Matrimonio* is bright, severe, and flashy.

Your friend

N.

(48) To Franziska Nietzsche

Pension Neptun, Zürich, October 4, 1884

My dear Mother:—In the meantime you will probably have been informed in all detail that your children have again made up nicely and are of *good cheer* in every respect. How long this togetherness, however, is to last no one can say yet as of this date. The labors I intend to carry out will under all circumstances soon make me seek seclusion. But the clubfoot I am dragging around, meaning the 104 kilograms of my books, won't let me fly too far from here.—

For this year at least *our* visiting together is, thus, not going to be possible. I wish with all my heart that you may not take it too hard.

The good intention which you express in your last letter to have me walk the earth somewhat more sumptuously *dressed*, I accept with many thanks. As a matter of fact, I am rather indigent and, owing to changing my habitations so often, a little shabby, like a mountain sheep.

My health gives me trouble all the time. A strange city and things I am not used to in diet, and a different daily routine always will play havoc with me. My appearance, however, is good and not any different than last year.

With cordial thanks,

Thine   F.

(49) To Elisabeth Nietzsche

Zürich, October 22, 1884

Yesterday, my dear Llama, was a beautiful day, and your letter came to hand amidst all sorts of good things. Beginning early the weather was brilliantly magnificent, as is customary in Nice. At nine o'clock I went to the concert hall and refreshed myself on Beethoven and Bizet. Then the German proprietor of the *Hôtel des Etrangers* conveyed to me in the most deferential manner his joy over the fact that I had contemplated to stay in his house for the winter and guaranteed the same conditions under which I stayed till now in Nice. Next, Hegar came and brought Gast's score. Every fall he puts himself and his orchestra at disposal and of his own accord he offered Peter Gast to cede him half an hour of each of his own orchestra recitals, thus affording Gast an opportunity to "take charge" of the orchestra himself and rehearse his own work. *After* he had made this offer I told him of Gast's request, which he had already fulfilled, to be near Hegar and thus live in close

110

proximity to an orchestra. In brief, all tied in very well, and I believe I have *promoted* Gast's destiny by staying here at Zürich.

In the afternoon I took a long walk with my new friend, Helene Druscowicz who lives with her mother just a few doors away from the *Pension Neptun*. Of all womenfolk I have come to know it is she who has occupied herself by far the most seriously with my books, and not without benefit. Investigate once how you like her last writings (*Three English Poetesses*, Eliot among them whom she adores much, and a book on Shelley). At present she is translating the English poet Swinburne. She seems to be a noble and upright creature who does not treat my "philosophy" damagingly. I wish you would read the novels of Miss Glogau, my admirer in Berlin; she is highly spoken of because of her "psychological sensitivity."

In the evening I went to the first concert in the concert hall to which Hegar had invited me, and thus I spent the evening of this fine day with *Arlésienne* and laid myself to sleep. This morning arrived a cordial and extremely discreet letter from my old friend Overbeck principally giving expression to his undivided joy over the fact that I have not lost "such a portion of loyal and genuine devotion as is mine in my mother and sister."—Since I did not have your addresses while *en route,* I sent you a letter to Naumburg.

Loyally yours,

F.

Long live independence! This is my daily thought. Have nothing to do with getting married!

(50) To Franziska and Elisabeth Nietzsche

Nice, March 21, 1885
Saturday

At last, my dear ones, I have this to say. It's only this past hour that I have been able to give you news and information concerning what I intend to do this spring. *Zürich,* through a sudden decision of Gast, has been struck from the program. This morning he announced *that he absolutely could not stand it any longer there* and was on his way to *Venice.* Now, I *must have* a meeting with Gast as we have common plans. Venice, besides, is the most beautiful of all cities in the present condition of my eyes. But enough! I am greatly pleased over the turn of events which relieves me of travelling to Zürich.

Poor G(ast) had the same experiences in Zürich as I had had in Basel during my youth, that is to say, for about ten years of my youth. The climate of these cities is in contradiction to our *productive* abilities, and this continued botheration makes us *ill.* *This* aspect of Basel was a very great misfortune for me. Even today I am suffering from the terrible after-effects of this period (and shall never get rid of them again).

One has to pay heavily for one's ignorance. Had I dealt with medical, climatic and suchlike problems at the right time, instead of with Theognis and Diogenes Laertius, I would not have become this half-ruined human being.—

And thus one loses one's youth. Already I am beyond 40 and still immersed in the first experiments with what *now* is necessary, but what one *should* have had at least 20 years ago.—

As you can see, once more I am in somewhat better humor. The really important circumstance is, probably, that Lanzky is gone. He is a person *much* deserving of esteem and *very* devoted to me, but what does all this mean to me? His significance in my case amounted to what I call "cloudy weather," "German weather" and the like. By the way, there is at present no man alive for whom I could care a *great deal*. The men whom I like have been dead a long, long time, for instance, Abbé Galiani, or Henry Beyle, or Montaigne.

About my sister's future I have apprehensions. By that I mean, I do not quite believe in Dr. Förster's return to Paraguay. Europe is really not so small, and if one does not *wish* to live in Germany (and here I am of the same mind as he), one does not by any means as yet have to be so far afield. To be sure, thus far I have worked up little enthusiasm for "the German soul," but still less for the desire to maintain this "magnificent" race *pure*. On the contrary—

Pardon me, but you can see how cheerful I am. Perhaps we shall see each other again this year, but *not* in Naumburg. You know the place does not agree with me and has not a thing that finds response in my heart. I was not "born" there and never felt as if I were "at home" there.

Nice this winter is exceptionally less bright and dry. But I shall hardly be able to get away before end of March.

Lovingly and devotedly

F.

I forgot to thank you for your letter, my dear mother, which crossed mine. It never entered my mind to take anything "badly"—on the contrary.

(51) To Elisabeth Nietzsche

Address: General Delivery, Venice, April 1885

My dear, dear Llama:—To tell you the truth, everything is very astounding to me, for instance, that, without ado you enter a relationship with a strange man and even want to go with him to the far corners of the earth. Now, I have written immediately to Oberbeck, that is, in connection with Dürer's leaf which, I feel, looks much too dark. Also, I want to send you the copy of my *Zarathustra* in the colorful private Persian edition—you can set it up as a fetish somewhere in some American jungle. Furthermore, I am sending you and Dr. Förster at the same time two copies of the fourth part with the express request that not a word be breathed to anyone about this fourth part and it be kept a secret as if *not* in existence. If, at some later date, the question becomes urgent what in particular is to be taken along to your new home, I would like to have the privilege of getting for you something that proves most necessary as a sort of "wedding present *post festum.*" Is not the Schmeitzner affair taking a turn which permits me the daring hope to even give presents? First of all, of course, there will be my printer C. G. Naumann who demands 284 *Marks* and 40 *Pfennige* from me.

Your propositions regarding the future do not resound too badly on my sounding board. I do not know how to thank you enough for including in them thoughts concerning myself. I counter with the observation that, perhaps, all worries about my future may stop abruptly. In the forenoon I tolerate my existence; but hardly so in the afternoon and evening. I even have the impression that under unfavorable

114

circumstances I have done enough to warrant my shaking the dust from my feet with honors.—And one more thing, I am becoming too blind to permit myself much reading and writing. Enough enters my mind almost daily for German professors to write two thick volumes about. But there is no one among my acquaintances for whom this stuff is suitable. There is so much amongst it that is impermissible: it hurts the others.

I confess that I would gladly give a lecture here or there, quite in the proper and approved manner as a moralist and great "educator" who is not a fool. But, students are so stupid and professors are even dumber! And, where should I give them? In Jena? For the moment I know of no place where I would like to be, Venice excepted, only the high moisture content of the air, 90%, plays havoc with me. Nice and the Upper Engadin are very dry.

By the way, I am *touched* that you have chosen the 22nd of May as your wedding day. I can't get rid of the feeling that in every possible respect you have *settled* and domiciled yourself where I dwelled some time previously. All you do is, for me, reminiscence, echo. As for myself, I have run away awfully far and have no longer anyone to whom I would even want to tell *where*. By no means believe that my son Zarathustra voices *my* opinions. He is one of my preparations and an interlude.—Please forgive me!

Gersdorff will go to Switzerland in summer in company of his sick wife. To my great astonishment Lanzky wrote a short while ago a long letter of thanks to my address here like a man who has become completely transformed. And I am supposed to be responsible for it! Thus, my efforts this past winter have not been in vain, as others have been.—

An old Dutchman from Haarlem sent me a testimonial in homage saying "that, after the death of Schopenhauer, I" etc.—People don't know and don't get enough of a scent as to *where* I am bound for. I am a dangerous animal and am ill suited to veneration.

The academic society in Basel has once again renewed my 1000 *franc* pension for three more years. Likewise have the 1000 *francs* of the Heusler Foundation been granted me once more by the regents of the university. The contribution of 1000 *francs* which the state made will stop at the end of this year, not as early as June, and it is hardly probable that it will be renewed. This is how "matters" stand.

I answered our dear mother right after receiving her good parcel. What fine shirts! What good honey! Please thank her once more in my name.—I do not know where to go this summer. A deep forest would be best, but there should be joyful people there who do not place me under the necessity of being on my guard.—All those who rave about "the emancipation of women" have slowly, ever so slowly, come to realize that I am their "bad animal." In Zürich the women students burst into a great rage against me. *Finally!*—and *how* many of these "at lasts" do I have to look forward to?!

In love,

Thy Brother

Rooming here has been terrible. I have moved and now it is even worse. There is no one who bothers himself with these things. Oh Genoa, oh Nice!

Heavens above! I ought to have the first three *Zarathustras* myself! Please, therefore, send me *without delay* the three sections from stock at Naumburg. As already said, you will receive *my* copy.

(52) To Bernhard and Elisabeth Förster (Nietzsche)

Nice, after Christmas 1885

My Dear Ones:—The weather is magnificent, and so
your animal must once again put on a glad countenance despite the fact that he has experienced quite
melancholy days and nights. Nevertheless, Christmas
turned out to be a feast day. Your letter reached me
at noon. Quickly the chain was put 'round the neck
and the cute little calendar went in hiding into the
vest pocket. But in the process, unfortunately, the
"money" dropped out, provided—as our dear mother
wrote—there was money in the letter. Forgive your
blind animal for opening his mail on the street. It
could well have been that something slipped out,
for I was looking very anxiously for the letter. Let's
hope a poor little old woman was around and thus
found her "little Christ Child" in the street.

Later I went to my peninsula St. Jean, walked a
long way around the coast, and finally sat down
among a group of young soldiers who were bowling.
In the hedges fresh roses and geraniums, and everything was verdant and warm, not at all Nordic. Then
your animal drank three glasses, quite large, of a
sweet country wine and was nearly a li'le tipsy. At
least I began to address the waves when they came
rushing on too boisterously as you say to the chickens
"shoo! shoo!" After that I rode back to Nice and
supped royally at my boarding house. A large Christmas tree also was lit. Just imagine, I discovered a
boulanger de luxe who knows what a cheese pie is.
He told me that the King of Württemberg had or-
dered one for his birthday. This came to my mind as
I was writing the word "royally."—

I was sick for a few days. Hence the letter was

117

left unfinished. In the meantime, Overbeck wrote that Rohde was called to Leipzig. Will he accept the call? Oddly enough it moves me to think that now everybody congregates in Leipzig or vicinity and I get the feeling as if I shall not be entirely without a home. Actually, it was nice in Leipzig this fall also, a bit melancholic, but just as people like ourselves find all enjoyments in life—spiced with a wee old rose scent of the *unreturnable.*

Sooner or later my eyes will hold out only in the forests. Still, *old friends* must live near such forests. All in all, does this not spell "Rosental"? And, at last, one has declared war on *Knoblauch* by decision of the Leipzig Council (the only form of anti-Semitism sweet-smelling to your cosmopolitan rhino)—forgive me!

Love as anciently

Your   F.

Heavens above! I forgot to wish you *an awful lot of luck* and good health and fortitude and good thoughts and loyal human beings this coming year!—

N.B. Once again I have learned to sleep (without soporifics).

(53) To Malwida von Meysenbug

Sils-Maria, September 24, 1886

My dear Friend:—My last day in Sils-Maria. All birds have already flown away. The sky "darkling" as in fall, the cold increasing,—therefore the "hermit of Sils-Maria" must be on his way.

I sent greetings yet everywhere as someone closing his yearly account with his friends also. While so occupied it crossed my mind that you have not had a letter from me for a long time. A request for your address in Versailles which I had made by letter to Miss B. Rohr in Basel, went, unfortunately, unfulfilled. Thus I am sending these lines to Rome to where I also addressed a book a short while ago. Its title is *Beyond Good and Evil, Prelude to a Philosophy of the Future.* (I beg your pardon! By no means should you read it, less yet tell me your feelings about it. Let us assume that it *may* be read toward the year 2000 . . .)

Let me thank you cordially for your kind enquiry of my mother from whom I had news this spring. I just was in a bad way. The heat to which I, a neighbor to glaciers, was no longer accustomed, nearly crushed me. Add to this that I get the sensation in Germany as if nothing but hostile winds are blowing in my face without feeling the least inclination or obligation to blow *back*. It is simply the wrong environment for me. What concerns the Germans of today does not concern *me*,—which is, of course, no reason to bear ill will towards them.—

Now, then, old man Liszt who knew how to live and how to die, permitted himself at last, as it were, to be *buried* in the Wagnerian cause and world, as

119

if he belonged quite inevitably and inseparably. This hurt me right into Cosima's soul. It is one of the falsehoods the more around Wagner, one of those almost insurmountable misunderstandings under which Wagner's fame grows today and runs to foliage. To judge by what I have thus far learned about Wagner's followers, the present-day "Wagonwrighting" (*Wagnerei*) seems to me to be an unconscious drawing closer to Rome, which is the same, seen from within, that Bismarck does from without.

Even my old friend Malwida—oh! you do not know her!—is basically Catholic in all her instincts, to which, believe it or not, belongs the indifference toward formulas and dogmas. Only an *ecclesia militans* requires intolerance. Every deep composure and positive faith *permits* scepticism, gentleness towards others and other things.

To finish off I shall copy a few words about myself which are to be read in the *Bund* for the 16th and 17th of September. Title: "Nietzsche's Dangerous Book."

"Those piles of dynamite which were used in the building of the St. Gotthardt line were marked with black flags warning of the danger to life.— Entirely in the same sense do we speak of the new book by the philosopher Nietzsche as of a *dangerous* book. This designation is not meant by us to carry any trace of blame against the author and his work, as little as that black flag is meant to censure the explosive. Still less would it occur to us to hand this lonely thinker over to the pulpit crows and altar ravens by calling attention to the dangerousness of his book. The spiritual explosive, just as the material one, can serve a very useful purpose. It is not necessary that it be used with criminal intentions. Let it be said merely that it is well to state explicitly where such material is stored, '*Here lies dynamite!*'"

Please, dear friend, be nice and grateful to me if I keep a little *distance* from you! . . . and make no effort to lure you on to *my* paths and "*detours.*" For, to again quote the *Bund:*

"Nietzsche is the first one who knows a new way around, but such a fearful one that one really becomes frightened on seeing him walking along that lonely path untrodden till now! . . ."

Well, in brief, greetings to you from the *hermit* of Sils-Maria.
Address, for the time being: General Delivery, Genoa.

(54) To Gottfried Keller

Ruta ligure, October 14, 1886

Highly Revered Sir:—Meanwhile I have taken the liberty, following an old liking and custom, to send you my latest book; at least my publisher Naumann was so instructed. Perhaps this book full of question marks offends your taste, possibly its *form* does not. Whoever has seriously and with a biased heart taken trouble with the German language must, it seems to me, mete out a little justice to me: It *is* quite an accomplishment to have sphinxlike and stillborn problems such as those raised by me, speak forth.—

Last spring my aged mother begged me to read her your epigrams and we both blessed you from the bottom of our heart (also from our full throat, for we laughed so much), for the taste of that honey was so pure, so fresh and gritty.

Permit me to express once again my loyalty to you and my veneration.

Yours,
Prof. Dr. Friedrich Nietzsche

(55) To Hans von Bülow

(Venice, October 22, 1887)

Dear Sir:—There was a time when you pronounced the most justifiable sentence of death possible *in rebus musicis et musicantibus* over one of my pieces of music. In spite of it all, I have the courage to send you something again, a hymn to life which I wish all the more to *remain alive*. It is to be sung sometime in the future, be that future near or distant, in my memory, in memory of a philosopher who knew no present and really never desired to live in the present. Does he *merit* that?

Above all, could it be that also as a musician I have *learned* something?

My very dear Sir, I remain yours with unchanged sentiments,

Dr. Fr. Nietzsche

Address: *Pension de Genève*, Nice, France.

(56) To Erwin Rohde   Nice, November 11, 1887

Dear Friend, it seems I still have to make good whatever I have done to you this spring. As a token that I am not lacking in good will I am sending you herewith a publication which just came out (perhaps I actually owe it to you, for it stands in very close connection with the one I sent you last). No, please don't let yourself be so easily alienated from myself! With my age, and in my isolation at least, I myself am not losing any more the few people in whom I put trust once.

                         Thine   N.

Nota bene. Concerning M. Taine I beg of you to come to your senses. Such rude things as you are saying and thinking about him irritate me. I would forgive Prince Napoleon for it, but *not* my friend Rohde. Anyone who misunderstands this kind of austere and magnanimous spirit (today T. is the educator of all the more earnest scientific men in France), I cannot easily believe will understand something of my own task. Honestly, you never said a word which would lead me to suspect that you *know* what destiny rests upon me. Did I ever blame you for it? Not even in my heart, and be it only for the reason that I am not at all used to it from anyone else. Who, till now, has shown me the kindness of approaching me with even a particle of passion and suffering? Has anyone had even a glimmer of the true cause of my long and protracted illness which I may nonetheless have conquered at last? I now have 43 years behind me and am still fully as alone as when I was a child.—

(57) To Georg Brandes

Dear Sir:—A couple of readers whom one personally holds in esteem, but otherwise no readers, that, indeed, would correspond to what I want. As concerns the latter part of this wish, I must confess I see more clearly as I go along that it will remain unfulfilled. I am the more happy in that in order *satis sunt pauci* the *pauci* are not missing and never have remained away. Among those living (naming only the ones you know) I mention my excellent friend Jacob Burckhardt, Hans von Bülow, H. Taine, the Swiss poet Keller. Of those who have passed on I mention the old Hegelian Bruno Bauer and Richard Wagner. I am sincerely glad that such a fine European and cultural missionary as you yourself also wants to belong to them. I thank you deeply from my heart for this intention.

To be sure, you will run into trouble in this undertaking. I myself have no doubt in my mind that my writings are still "very much German" in one or the other respect. Doubtlessly you will sense this much more strongly, spoiled as you are by yourself,—I mean by the captivating free and French manner in which you handle the language (a somewhat more sociable manner in comparison with mine). Many words I am using have incrusted themselves with foreign salts and taste differently to my tongue than they will to my readers. More yet. In the range of my experiences and conditions the rarer, more distant, finer scales preponderate over the normal, middle-of-the-road ones. To speak as an old musician, which I really am, I also have an ear for

124

quarter tones. Finally—and it is this which, probably most of all, makes my books dark—I possess an instinctive distrust of dialectics, even of reasons. I seem to care more for the courage, the degree of bravery exemplified in what a man already considers "true" or not yet "true" . . . (I myself rarely display the valor to acknowledge what I really know.)

The expression "aristocratic radicalism" which you are using is very good. If you permit me, this is the most intelligent word I have thus far read about myself.

How far this mode of thinking has already carried me in thought, how far it will yet lead me, I almost am afraid to prognosticate. Yet there are roads which do not let us go any other way; and thus I am going ahead because I *must* go forward.

In order not to neglect on my part to mention what could make your access to my cave, that is to say, my philosophy, easier, my publisher in Leipzig has been instructed to send you my earlier writings *en bloc*. I would especially recommend reading the new prefaces (the books have nearly all been edited anew). These prefaces could, if read in sequence, perhaps throw some light on me, provided I am not dark myself (dark in and for myself) as *obscurissimus obscurorum virorum* . . .

This could, of course, be quite possible.

Are you a musician? Just now they are publishing a choral work by myself, a "Hymn to Life." This, of all the music I have composed, is fated to remain and to be sung sometime "in my memory," provided that otherwise also enough of my things survive. You can see with what kind of posthumous thoughts I am living. But a philosophy, such as mine, is like a grave,—one no longer lives contemporaneously with others. *Bene vixit qui bene latuit;* these are the words on Descartes' tombstone. A funereal inscription, no doubt!

I, too, wish I could meet you sometime.

Your

Nietzsche

N.B. For the duration of this winter I shall remain in Nice. My address in summer is Sils-Maria, Upper Engadin, Switzerland. I have given up my professorship at the university. I am three quarters blind.

(58) To Carl von Gersdorff

Pension de Genève, Nice (France)
December 20, 1887

Dear Friend:—Rarely in my life did a letter bring me so much joy as yours of November 30th. It would seem to me that, with it, all that is between ourselves has again most honestly and thoroughly been arranged in good order. Such happiness could hardly have been saved me for a more suitable point in time than the present one. Just now my life has reached in a very special sense the *full noonday.* One door shuts, another is opening. What I have done in recent years was only a settling of accounts, a closing of the books, the adding of that which is past. At long last I am done with man and thing and have drawn a line under the whole account. *Who* and *what* shall remain with me—at this juncture where I must (am condemned to) press onward to the real core of my existence—that is the capital problem of the moment. For, *entre nous,* the tension under which I am living, the pressure of a great task and passion, are too great for persons new to me who wish to seek propinquity with me now. In fact, the emptiness around me is tremendous. I really stand only those who are total strangers and whose acquaintance I make accidentally, in addition, of course, to those who belong to me from olden times and from childhood. All the rest have crumbled away, or have been cast off (there was much that was violent and painful while that was going on).

I was moved when I received at this particular time as a present your letter and your old friendship expressed therein. Something similar happened this past summer when *Deussen* suddenly appeared in the Engadin, Deussen whom I had not seen for 15 years (he is the first professor of philosophy who is a persuaded follower of *Schopenhauer* and maintains that I am the cause of his transformation). I am likewise deeply grateful for all I owe the *maëstro* of Venice. I visit him almost every year and may tell you without exaggeration that *in rebus musicis et musicantibus* he is my only hope, my consolation and my pride. For he has, as it were, grown out of me. What he now produces in the way of music is far above everything that is being composed these days, be it in depth and kindness of soul as well as classic taste. I am *not* contradicting myself when I say that people behave coolly and indecently toward him and he has for long years experienced real torture by rejections, lack of tact and German boorishness. But this is the moral of history: One either perishes by life's tribulations or *emerges the stronger because of them.*

You also, my dear old friend, thou much-tried one, will be able to subscribe to this sentence, won't you?

It seems to me that I am writing you presently a *birthday letter,* am I correct? The same as in the past, in our "good, old times?" (I have, in truth, never for a moment been disloyal to you; tell this also to your dear wife besides giving her my compliments.)

Anciently in love and friendship

Thine

Nietzsche

Just now *The Hymn to Life,* Composed by Friedrich Nietzsche, was published by E. W. Fritzsch. It is for mixed choir and orchestra and is scored.—Please read, I implore you, the *new* edition of *The Gay Science.* There is something in there to cause you to laugh.

(59) To Georg Brandes   Nice, February 19, 1888

Dear Sir:—You have most pleasantly obliged me with your contribution to the concept "modernity." For this winter especially I have been circling high and wide around this most important question of value, very much in upper regions, much like a bird and with the best of intentions of looking down on what is modern with as much of a nonmodern spirit as possible . . . I admire, I must confess, your tolerance in making, as much as your reserve in with-holding, judgments. How you suffer all these "little children" and forbid them not to come unto you. Even Heyse!—

For my next trip to Germany I have planned oc-cupying myself with the psychological problem of Kierkegaard and, likewise, to renew my acquaintance with your older literature. In the best sense of the word this will be for *my benefit* and will serve me to "bring home to me" my own obduracy and arro-gance in judgment.

Yesterday my publisher sent me a telegram telling me that the books have been forwarded to you. I shall spare you and me the tale why this happened so late. Dear sir, please be of good cheer though the jig is up, I mean this Nietzschean literature.

I myself am conceited enough to believe that I have given the "new Germans" the richest, *most ex-perienced,* and the most independent books they have, barring none. And so far as I personally am concerned I believe that I am a tremendous happen-ing in the crisis of value judgments. However, this could be an error and, moreover, even stupidity. I wish I did not *have to* believe anything regarding myself.

Just a few remarks to boot. You have reference to my first productions (the *Juvenilia* and *Juvenalia*). Very well.

The pamphlet against Strauss, the horselaugh of a "very free thinker" over one who thinks he is one, caused a tremendous scandal. I was then already *Prof. ordin.* in spite of my 27 years, hence a sort of authority and something that has *proven* itself. The most naive statements about this incident in which nearly every *person of note* took sides for or against me and a ridiculous quantity of paper was covered with print, are to be found in Karl Hillebrand's *Times, Nations and Men,* vol. 2. The great event assumed this magnitude not because I jeered at the senile concoctions of an extraordinary critic, but because I caught German taste unawares and *in flagrante* while committing an act of compromising bad taste. In other words, as of one mind, they had admired Strauss' "old and new faith" as a masterpiece of freedom and refinement of spirit (likewise of style!) despite all differences in religious and theological persuasions. My pamphlet was the first assassination of German culture (that "culture" which they say with pride bore the victory over France). The word which I coined, *Bildungsphilister,* remained in the language after the discussion raged furiously to and fro.

The two pamphlets about Schopenhauer and Richard Wagner represent, as I see it now, more self-confessions, above all pledges to myself than real psychological investigations of these masters who were as deeply related to me as they were my antagonists. (I was the first who distilled a sort of unity from both. Now this superstition you will find very much in the foreground of German culture. All followers of Wagner are disciples of Schopenhauer. When I was young it was different. At that time it was the last "Hegelings" who were on the side of Wagner, and the watchword of even the fifties was still "Wagner and Hegel.")

Between *Untimely Meditations* and *Human, All-too Human* there lie a crises and a shedding of skin. Even physiologically I was living for years in the closest vicinity of death. This turned out to be a great good fortune: I forgot myself, I survived myself . . . The same trick I accomplished once more later.

Thus, we have been giving presents one to the other, a couple of wanderers—may I presume?—who are glad they encountered each other.

I remain

Yours devotedly

Nietzsche

(60) To Georg Brandes

General Delivery, Turin (Italy)
April 10, 1888

But, my dear Sir, what a surprise!—Where did you gather the courage to want to talk about a *vir obscurissimus* in public! . . . Are you under the impression that I am known in my dear fatherland? There they are treating me as if I were some curiosity and absurdity, something one does not, for the time being, have to *take seriously* . . . Apparently you have gotten wind of the fact that I myself am not taking them seriously either. And why should I in this day and age when "German spirit" has become a *contradictio in adjecto!* For the photograph I am deeply appreciative. Unfortunately, there is nothing of the sort of me. The last pictures which I owned, my sister who is married and lives in South America took with her.

131

I am appending a small *Vita*, the first I have written.

Concerning the periods during which I wrote the individual volumes, they are listed on the back page of *Beyond Good and Evil*. Do you still have that leaf?

The Birth of Tragedy was written between the summer of 1870 and the winter of 1871 (and finished in Lugano where I lived together with the family of Field Marshal Moltke).

The *Untimely Meditations* written between 1872 and summer 1875 (they were meant to be 13 in all; luckily my health said no!).

I am very glad over what you say about *Schopenhauer as an Educator*. This small pamphlet serves me as a sign of recognition. To whom it tells nothing *personal*, he surely will have also otherwise nothing to do with me. Basically I have incorporated in it the routine according to which I have lived up to now. It is a serious *promise*.

Human, All-too Human, together with the two appendices, summer 1876 to 1879. *The Dawn*, 1880. *The Gay Science,* January 1882. *Zarathustra*, 1883 to 1885 (each part was written in about ten days. Perfect condition of one who is "inspired." Everything was conceived while strenuously on the march. Absolute certainty, as if every sentence had been called out to me. Simultaneously while writing it down very great bodily elasticity and fulness—).

Beyond Good and Evil, summer of 1885, in the Upper Engadin, and during the winter following in Nice.

The Genealogy was finished, gotten in shape and sent to press in Leipzig ready to be typeset between the 10th and 30th of July 1887. (Of course, there are also *philologica* by my pen. But with that both of us have no longer anything to do.)

Just now I am giving Turin a trial. I want to stay here till the 5th of June and go to the Engadin afterwards. The winter is hard and has been bad up to now. But the city is superbly quiet and flatters my instincts. The most beautiful pavement in the world.

Greetings from your grateful and devoted

Nietzsche

A pity I understand neither Danish nor Swedish.

Vita. I was born the 15th of October 1844, on the battlefield of Lützen. The first name I heard was that of Gustav Adolf. My ancestors were Polish noblemen (Nïezky). It seems the type is well preserved despite three German "mothers." In foreign countries I usually am considered a Pole; even this winter the roster of foreign visitors in Nice entered me *comme Polonais.* They tell me that my head may be found in the paintings of Matejko's. My grandmother belonged to the Schiller-Goethe circle in Weimar. Her brother became the successor of Herder in the office of Commissary-general of Weimar. I had the good fortune of having been a pupil at the venerable *Schulpforta* from where so many have gone forth who are of account in German literature (such as Klopstock, Fichte, Schlegel, Ranke and so on and so forth). We had teachers who would have done honor to any university (or have done so). I went to university at Bonn, later at Leipzig. The old Ritschl, then the first philologist of Germany, recognized my abilities almost from the start. At 22 years I became collaborator of the *Literarische Zentralblatt* (Zarncke). I was responsible for founding the philological society in Leipzig, which is still in existence. In winter 1868-69 the University of Basel offered me a professorship; I did not even have my doctorate yet. The University of Leipzig bestowed upon me the doctorate afterwards, in a very dignified manner, without any examination whatever, even without a dissertation. From Easter 1869 to 1879 I lived at Basel. I was forced to give up my German citizenship since, as commissioned officer (mounted artillery) I would have been called up too often and disturbed in my academic activities. Nevertheless, I am familiar with two weapons, sabre and cannon, and, perhaps, even with a third one . . . Everything was going very well in Basel, my youth notwithstanding. It happened that particularly when the doctor's degree was being granted the examined person was older than the examiner. I was very much favored by virtue of the fact that a cordial rapprochement existed between Jacob Burckhardt and myself, something unusual with this rather hermitlike thinker who likes to live apart from other persons. Fortune smiled even more on me in that, right from the beginning of my stay in Basel, I became indescribably intimate and closely associated with Richard and Cosima Wagner who then lived on their country estate Triebschen, near Luzern, as on an island and severed from all earlier relationships. For several years we experienced in common all great and little things. Confidence without reserve governed our relationship. (You will find in print in the collected writings of Wagner, vol. VII, an epistle of his addressed to me on the occasion of *The Birth of Tragedy*.) Through these connections I came to know a large circle of interesting men (and "women"), actually almost everything that thrives between Paris and Petersburg. Toward 1876 my health grew worse. At that time I spent a winter in Sorrento with my old friend, the Baroness Meysenbug (*Memoirs of an Idealist*), and the sympathetic Dr. Rée. I did not improve. An extremely painful and persistent head malady developed which exhausted all my strength. During long years it became aggravated till it reached its highest point in a habitual state of pain so that the year would have 200 painful days in it. The illness must have had an entirely local origin, every neuropathological basis was completely absent. I have never had any symptoms of mental derangement, not even fever or fainting spells. My pulse at the time was as slow as that of Napoleon I (*i.e.,* 60). I developed a specialty consisting in bearing up under the extreme pain *cru, vert* with perfect lucidity of mind for two or three days in a row, vomiting continually mucus. Some have been spreading the rumor that I was confined to a lunatic asylum (even died in it). Nothing is more erroneous. My mind actually did mature during that dreadful period. Witness *The Dawn* which I wrote in 1881, during a winter of unbelievable misery in Genoa, removed from physicians, friends and relatives. That book is a sort of "dynamometer" for me; I wrote it with a minimum of vigor and health. Beginning 1882 I improved again, albeit very slowly. The crisis had been weathered (my father died very young, exactly in the year of his life in which I myself was closest to death). Still today it is necessary for me to exercise extreme caution. A few conditions of a climatic and meteorological nature are indispensable to my health. It is not by choice but by necessity that

I spend the summers in the Upper Engadin, the winters at the Riviera . . . In the final analysis the illness was of the greatest service to me: it lifted me out of myself and gave me back the courage to be myself . . . Then, too, I am according to my instincts a brave animal, yes, a military one. The long resistance has somewhat exasperated my pride.—Am I a philosopher?—But what of it! . . .

(61) To Peter Gast

Turin, Thursday
(May 31, 1888)

If I answer you again immediately you will be left without guessing what I lack—that is, that *you* are missing, dear friend! However much spring is to my liking, it does not bring me the best of things, that which even the worst springs have brought thus far —your music! The sound of your music is linked with my concept of "spring"—since Recoaro!—just about in the same manner as the tender pealing of the bells above the city of the lagoons is with my concept of "Easter." As often as one of your melodies comes to my mind, I remain enmeshed in these reminiscences with a gratitude that is long-lasting. Through nothing have I experienced as much rebirth, elevation and relief as through your music. It is my *good* music *par excellence* for which I always get into neater clothes inside than for any other.

Day before yesterday I took the liberty of sending you theatrical notices of Dr. Fuchs. There is much that is excellent and of living experience in it.

Dr. Brandes' lectures have terminated in a beautiful manner, with a big ovation of which Brandes, however, maintains it was not meant for him. He assured me that my name is now popular in all intellectual circles of Kopenhagen and is known throughout Scandinavia. It has the appearance as if my problems were of great interest to these northern countries. In particular they were better prepared, for instance, for my theory of a "master morality" by virtue of their general and *exact* knowledge of the Icelandic sagas which furnish very rich material in support of it. I am glad to hear that the Danish philologists approve of my derivation of *bonus* and accept it. Considered in itself it is quite a feat to derive the concept "good" from the concept of "warrior." No philologist would ever have been able to hit upon such an idea without the presuppositions I furnished.—

It is truly a pity that you have not yet made an excursion into the Cadoric Alps instead of into paper-blacking. My bad example patently spoils your manners which are naturally much better. The weather has been very suitable for such a mountain exploration. I myself have not made any use of it and am similarly dissatisfied with myself on that account.

To the weeks just past I owe a basic *lesson*. I found the lawbook of *Manu* in a French translation, which was compiled in India under strict surveillance of highly placed native priests and scholars. This absolutely *Aryan* product, a priestly code of morals based on the Vedas, the caste-concept and very ancient traditions—*not* pessimistic, however much it is essentially priestly—supplements my ideas concerning religion in a most remarkable way. I get the

137

impression that everything else we possess in the way of great moral institutes of law, is an imitation and even caricature of it, the Egyptian one most of all. But even Plato seems to be merely *well instructed* by a Brahman in all his main points. The Jews appear in this matter like a Chaṇḍala race which has learned from its *masters* the principles according to which a *priesthood* assumes mastery and organizes a people . . . Also the Chinese appear to have produced their Confucius and Laotze with the knowledge of this classical, *most ancient law book*. The medieval organization looks like a queer attempt in the dark to regain all those ideas on which the ancient Indo-Aryan society is based, but adopting the *pessimistic* values which have their origin in the soil of racial *decadence.*—The *Jews* here also are mere "mediators,"—they do not invent anything.

So much, my dear friend, as a token of *how much I was delighted* to converse with you. Tuesday I shall depart from here.

Cordially,

Your

Nietzsche

(62) To Karl Knortz

My dear Sir:—The arrival, now two weeks ago, of two works by your pen for which I owe you thanks, seems to be an indication that in the meantime the literature I sent is in your possession. Your request to give you a picture of myself, be it as thinker, be it as author and poet, appears extraordinarily difficult to me. The first larger attempt of this kind was made last winter by the splendid Dane, Dr. Georg Brandes, who may be known to you as a historian of literature. This man organized under the title of "The German Philosopher Friedrich Nietzsche" quite a long series of lectures on me at the university in Kopenhagen, whose success must have been very fine, to judge by what has been written me from there. He was able to awaken a lively interest in an audience of 300 persons in the audacity with which I pose my problems, and, as he himself states, has popularized my name throughout the northern countries. Otherwise I have a rather more secretive audience and circle of admirers to whom also some Frenchmen like M. Taine belong. It is my inmost conviction that these problems of mine, this my entire position as an "immoralist" is much too premature for the times, much too unprepared. As for myself, the thought of making propaganda for it is quite distant from my mind. Thus far I have not moved a finger in that direction.

As concerns my *Zarathustra* I believe that it is just about the deepest book that exists in the German language, also the one linguistically most perfect. However, to have such a mutual, *sympathetic understanding* we need whole generations who must first run through those inner experiences which were necessary to produce this work. I would almost advise anyone to begin with my last works which are the most extensive and important (*Beyond Good and Evil* and *Toward A Genealogy of Morals*). To me, personally, the most sympathetic are my middling books, *The Dawn* and *The Gay Science*. They are also the most personal ones.

The *Untimely Meditations*, youthful writings in a certain sense, are deserving of greatest attention for tracing my development. In *Times, Nations and Men* by Karl Hillebrand you will find a couple of good essays about the first "Untimely Ones." My publication against Strauss caused a great storm. The publication on Schopenhauer whose reading I recommend especially, shows how an energetic and instinctively affirmative spirit knows how to receive the most beneficent stimuli even from a pessimist. For a few years which belong to the most valuable ones of my life, I was deeply confiding in Richard Wagner and Cosima Wagner and on most intimate terms with them. If I am now among the *opponents* of the Wagnerian movement it is, let it be understood as a matter of course, not from paltry motives. In the collected works of Wagner's, vol. IX (if I remember correctly), you may read a letter addressed to me which bears witness of our relationship.

I am so conceited as to say that my books are of the first order of magnitude by virtue of a wealth of psychological experiences, intrepidity in the face of greatest danger, and lofty candor. I shun no comparison with respect to the art of presentation and artistic demands. A long cherished love binds me to the German language, a covert intimacy, a deep veneration, a sufficient reason for reading hardly any books which are being written in this language.

Please accept, my dear Sir, the best greetings of
Professor Dr. Nietzsche

(63) To Paul Deussen

Sils-Maria, September 14, 1888
Address until November 15th: General
Delivery, Turin, Italy

Dear Friend:—I do not like to leave Sils without pressing your hand once more in memory of the *greatest* surprise which this summer abounding in surprises has brought me. Then, too, I can now again talk more bravely than when I had to answer you. Health has since returned *along with* the "better" weather (for the concept "good" is impractical for meteorologists and philosophers). To be sure, the week just past we had the real *superfluidy* of the whole year, a veritable deluge which caused the most serious flood distress situations in the Upper and Lower Engadin. In four days there was a precipitation of 220 millimeters while the normal amount for a whole month here is 80 millimeters.—

You will receive a package this month yet, a small esthetic polemical treatise in which I for the first time and in an uncompromising manner throw light on the *psychological problem of Wagner*. It is a declaration of war, no quarter given, against the entire movement. In the last analysis I am the only one who possesses breadth and depth enough not to be unsure of himself.—That one of my literary productions, a pamphlet if you will, *against* Wagner will cause a certain sensation I already gather from the last report of my publisher. Merely on the basis of the advance notice in the journal of the book trade so many orders have been received that the edition of a thousand copies may be regarded as exhausted (that is, if the copies which have been *asked for* will not at a later date instead of going out of the publisher's be finding their way back to him . . .). Please be so good as to read the pamphlet also from the point of view of taste and style. *No one in Germany today* writes like this. It would be just as easy to translate it into French as it would be difficult, nearly impossible, to translate it into German . . .

—There is already another manuscript at the publisher's which is a very concise and excellent expression of my whole *philosophical heterodoxy*—hidden under much pleasantness and malice. It is called *The Idling Psychologist.*—When all is said and done, *these two writings* are really only recreations in the midst of a tremendously difficult and decisive task which, *when rightly understood*, splits the history of mankind into two halves. Its meaning, expressed in four words, is "transvaluation of all values." When I am done much of what was debatable till now is *no longer debatable*. The realm of *tolerance* has been reduced by means of value judgments of the first order to mere cowardice and weakness of character. To be a *Christian*—to name but one result, will henceforth be considered *indecent*.—Much of this most revolutionary conversion of which the world shall know, is already going on and progressing inside me. The only drawback is, to say it once more, that I need every kind of recreation and pastime in order to produce the work without toil, as in play, an expression of the "freedom of the will." The *first* book of it is already half complete.—My dear old friend, you surely *have guessed* that there is much *to be printed* in this and the following years and that that strange generosity with money knocked on my door really at a *decisive and opportune moment*. It is necessary to possess *luck* for everything, even for doing good . . . A few years earlier—who knows *what* I might have answered you!—

With heartiest greetings,

Thine friend

Nietzsche

—I am also sending a copy to Barrister-at-law Volkmar.

(64) To Malwida von Meysenbug

Turin, October 18, 1888

My dear friend:—These are not matters in which I tolerate contradiction. In questions of *decadence* I am the highest court of appeal existing now on earth. These people of the present age with their lamentable depravity of instincts, should deem themselves lucky to possess someone who pours them clear wine in murkier cases. That Wagner knew how to create the belief in himself (as you express it with adorable innocence) as the "last expression of creative nature," as it were its "epilogue," that requires, indeed, *genius*, but a genius of the lie . . . I myself have the honor of being the reverse of it,—a genius of truth—

Friedrich Nietzsche

(65) To Malwida von Meysenbug

Turin, November 5, 1888

Just wait a little while, dearest friend! I shall yet furnish you the proof that *"Nietzsche est toujours baissable."* Without any doubt I have done you an injustice. But since I am suffering this fall from an overabundance of righteousness, it is a real treat for me to do an injustice . . .

The "Immoralist"

(66) To Meta von Salis

Turin, November 14, 1888

Dear Miss von Salis:—Inasmuch as I suffer chronically from an abundance of good humor and other blessings of fortune, you will in all likelihood excuse me for writing a completely senseless letter. Until now everything went better than well. I have pushed my load as if I were by nature an "immortal" coolie.

Not alone that the *first* book of the transvaluation was already finished on September 30th, in the meantime a quite incredible piece of literature with the title of *Ecce Homo, How to Become What One Is* has sprouted wings and, if not all indications deceive me, is now flying in the direction of Leipzig . . .

This *homo*, to be sure, is myself, including the *ecce*. In the attempt to spread a little light *and dread* about myself I seem to have been almost too successful. For instance, the last chapter has the unsavory heading: "Why I am a Destiny." That this is, indeed, the case is being proven so vigorously that in the end you remain squatting in front of me merely as a "larva," a mere "feeling breast."—That some *enlightenment* about myself was necessary has very recently been demonstrated by the case Malwida. I sent her, with some idea in the back of my mind, a copy of *The Case Wagner,* with the request to see whether she could not do something toward a good translation into French. "Declaration of War" against me—these were the words Malwida used.—

Once more, *entre nous,* I was able to convince myself that the famous "Idealism" in this case is basically an extreme form of lack of modesty, quite "innocent" as a matter of course. She was always permitted to put in a word and, it seems to me, nobody ever told her that with every sentence she not only errs but *lies* . . . "Beautiful souls," of course, will do just that, as they are not allowed to see reality. Spoiled all her life she is perched at last on her sofa like a funny little Pythia and says: "You are in error about Wagner! I know better! Exactly the same as *Michelangelo.*"—Thereupon I wrote her that Zarathustra wanted to do away with the good and just because they always *lie.* Upon that she answered that she was in perfect agreement with me, *because* there are so few really good persons . . .—And *that* served me as *defense* against Malwida for the time being.

Turin is not a place one forgets. Nice I have put in my files together with the romanticism of a Corsican winter. (It is no longer worth-while, those gentlemen, the bandits, have been really *done away with*, even the kings, the *Bellacoscia.*)—Fall here was a Claude Lorrain eternalized. Often I asked myself whether such a thing were possible here on earth. Curiously enough, against the miseries of summer *up there* there really was *compensation.* Here we are, the old God is still alive . . .

—People here, too, are *very nice* to me. My position has improved against that of spring to a degree I cannot figure out.—About my health I dare no longer speak, that is a point of view I have overcome.—The essay which I finished while yet in the Engadin, the most radical perhaps in existence, I gave the title of

The Twilight of the Idols
or, *How to Philosophize with the Hammer.*

They are done with printing.—If I reflect on what all I have committed between the 3rd of September and the 4th of November, I am afraid the earth will *tremble* very soon now. This time in Turin, two years ago, she did while I was in Nice, how *à propos*, in Nice. As a matter of fact, the last report of the observatory which came out yesterday already announced a slight tremor . . .

We had the experience of the dusky pomp of a *great* funeral. They carried one of the most venerable Piedmonteses, the Count of Robilant, to his grave. All

146

Italy was in mourning. They lost a Prime Minister whom they had been looking forward to impatiently, and whom no one can replace.

With devotion unparalleled,
Your

Nietzsche

Mr. Spitteler ejaculated a cry of *ecstasy* in the *Bund* about the *Case*.

(67) To Georg Brandes

Via Carlo Alberto 6, III, Turin
November 20, 1888

Dear Sir:—Please forgive me for answering right away. There occur now in my life *curiosa* of meaningfulness in chance which are absolutely unique. Day before yesterday for one, and now again.—Oh, if you only knew what I had just written when your letter called on me.—

With a cynicism which is destined to become world historical, I have now related myself. The book is called *Ecce Homo* and is an assassination without the least respect for the crucified one. It ends with thunder and lightning against everything Christian or infected by Christianity that you won't know any more where to turn or what to do. At last I am the first psychologist of Christianity and, old artillerist that I am can move up heavy guns the existence of which not even any opponent of Christianity had suspected in the least.—The whole is the prelude to the *Transvaluation of All Values*, the work which lies before me, finished. I swear to you, in two years we shall have the whole earth in convulsion. I am a destiny.—

Can you guess who comes off worst in *Ecce Homo?* The gentlemen, the Germans! I have told them terrible things . . . For example, the Germans have it on their conscience to have deprived the last *great* period of history, the Renaissance, of its meaning,— at a moment when the Christian values, the values of the decadence, had been defeated, when they had succumbed, even in the instincts of the highest clergy, in the face of counterinstincts, namely those of life. To *attack* the church,—that would be equivalent, don't you see, to reïnstituting Christianity.—(*Cesare Borgia* as Pope—that is the meaning of the Renaissance, its true symbol.)

—Further, you ought not to be angry over the fact that you yourself appear in a decisive place in the book—I just finished writing it—in connection with my stigmatizing the behavior of my German friends against me, that is, being completely left in the lurch as concerns honor and philosophy.—Enveloped in a pretty cloud of glory you suddenly make your appearance . . .

I have full faith in what you say about Dostoievski. From a different point of view I esteem him as the most valuable psychological material I know of. In a peculiar manner I am grateful to him however much he goes against my most basic instincts. About the same as my relationship to Pascal whom I almost love because he taught me a tremendous lot: The only *logical* Christian.

—Day before yesterday I read with rapture and as if I were at home, August Strindberg's *Les Mariés*.

148

My sincere admiration which is lessened nowise by my feeling to admire myself a little in the plot. Turin remains my residence.

Your Nietzsche, now a monstrous beast

Where may I send you my *The Twilight of the Idols?* No answer necessary if you remain another fortnight in Kopenhagen.

(68) To Carl Fuchs

Via Carlo Alberto 6, III, Turin
(December 18, 1888)

Dear Friend:—In the meantime everything is all right and proceeds wonderfully. Never did I even approximately experience such a time as from beginning September till today. The most unheard-of tasks are light, as in play. Health, like the weather, emerges daily with uncontrollable brightness and determination. I do not care to relate *what* all has been finished: *All is ready.*

The coming years will see the world upside down. After the old God has retired *I* shall henceforth govern the world.

No doubt my publisher has sent you *The Case* (*Wagner*) as well as quite recently *The Twilight of the Idols.* Are you not a little bit in a martial mood? I would greatly appreciate it if now a—*the*— genial musician would take publicly sides with me as an anti-Wagnerian and throw down the gauntlet to those in Bayreuth. A little brochure in which all

149

sorts of new and decisive statements were made about me, with application to a particular case, *music,*—what do you think of it? Nothing long drawn-out, something sensational, full of ready wit . . . The moment is auspicious. One *may* still say things that are true about me which two years later should become almost *niaiseries.*

—And *what* is Danzig doing, or, rather, *Not-Danzig?* . . . Relate yourself again to me, dear friend; I have time, I have ears . . .

The heartiest greetings to you

The Monstrous Beast

(69) To Franziska Nietzsche

Via Carlo Alberto 6, III, Turin
December 21, 1888

My aged Mother:—If I am not completely deceived, a few days hence is Christmas. Perhaps my letter will arrive in time yet as I am asking you to think of something that will give you pleasure and at the same time remind you pleasantly of your old creature, praying the while for indulgence because it is not *more.* (I hope Kürbitz understood the hint I gave him a few days ago.)

Here too the weather is a bit wintry, but not to the extent of my having to heat the room. As ever, the sun and the bright sky will triumph again after a few days of mist. We had a huge funeral, one of our Princes, the King's cousin, died. He did much for Italy, also for the navy, for he was Admiral of the Fleet.

In every respect I am glad to be done with Nice. Nevertheless, they sent me three cases with books here. Also, the only beneficent and amiable society in Nice which I used to enjoy there in the persons of the first-rate Köchlin family, nice people and accustomed to the best circles, was absent for the first time this winter. The old Köchlin is badly off; Madame Cécile wrote me in detail that it was persistent fever. They are in the neighborhood of Genoa at Nervi.—By contrast, I received good and cheering news from Geneva, from Madame Fynn and her Russian friend.

But the very best I hear from my friend *Gast* whose whole existence has changed wondrously. Not only do the foremost artists of Berlin, Joachim, de Ahna, take a very deep interest in his work, the kind of artist which Germany possesses and which is the most fastidious and pampered: Above all you would be astonished to know that he moves only in the wealthiest and most aristocratic circles of Berlin. It could be that his opera will see its first production in Berlin. Count Hochberg is intimately connected with the circles he frequents.

In truth, your old creature is now a tremendously famous animal. Not specially in Germany—for the Germans are too dense and too common for my spiritual height and have ever made fools of themselves on my account—but everywhere else. I have nothing but *select* natures among my admirers, all highly placed and influential persons, in St. Petersburg, in Paris, in Stockholm, in Vienna, in New York. Wish that you could know in what words top personages express their devotion to me, the most charming women, a Madame la Princesse Ténicheff by no means excluded. I have true geniuses among my admirers. Today there is no name which is treated with so much distinction and veneration as is mine.—Now you see, this is the trick: Without name, without rank, without wealth, I am being treated here like a little prince by everyone down to my street vendor who will not rest until she has picked out of all her grapes the sweetest.

Luckily, I am now equal to whatever the task confronting me demands. My health is actually excellent. The heaviest charges for which no man till now has proven himself strong enough, are easy for me.

My aged mother, please accept at the conclusion of this year my most cordial wishes and wish for me a year corresponding in every respect to the great events which are destined to take place in it.

Thine old Creature

(70) To Peter Gast

Turin, December 31, 1888

—You are right a thousand times! Please send warnings even to Fuchs . . . You will find in *Ecce Homo* a tremendous page on Tristan, as in general about my relationship to Wagner. Wagner is by all means the first name which occurs in *E. H.*—In things where I leave no doubt about anything I have also had the courage to go to extremes.

—Ah, Friend! *What* moment!—When your postal

arrived, *what* did I do then . . . It was the famous Rubicon . . .

—My address I no longer know. Let us assume that it could be for the time being the *Palazzo del Quirinale*.

N.

(71) To Peter Gast

(Cancellation: Turin, January 4, 1889)

To my maëstro Pietro.

Sing to me a new song: The world is transfigured and all the heavens are glad.
The Crucified One

(72) To Georg Brandes

(Cancellation: Turin, January 4, 1889)

To my friend Georg! After you discovered me it was no special feat to find me. The difficulty now is to lose me . . .

The Crucified One

(73) To Jacob Burckhardt

(Cancellation: Turin, January 4, 1889)

To my deeply respected Jacob Burckhardt.—This
was the jest on account of which I condone the bore-
dom of my having created a world. Now you are—
thou art—our great greatest teacher. For I, together
with Ariadne, have only to be the golden equilibrium
in all things. In every respect we have such as are
above us . . .

Dionysus

(74) To Cosima Wagner

(Beginning January 1889)

Ariadne, I love you.

Dionysus

(75) To Jacob Burckhardt

The 6th of January 1889
(Cancellation: Turin, January 5, 1889)

Dear Professor:—At long last I would much rather
be a Professor in Basel than God. But I did not dare
to carry my private egoism so far as to give up the
creation of the world on its account. You see, one
has to bring sacrifices, wherever and however one
lives.—Nevertheless, I have rented a small student
room opposite the *Palazzo Carignano* (in which I
was born as Vittorio Emanuele) which also permits

154

me to hear the splendid music in the *Galleria Subalpina* below me while sitting at my desk. I am paying 25 *francs* with service, am making my own tea and do all my errands myself. I am troubled by torn boots and thank heaven every moment for the *old* world for which mankind has not been simple and quiet enough.—Since I am condemned to entertain the next eternity with cracking bad jokes, I am occupied here with writing which leaves really nothing to be desired, is rather nice and not at all strenuous. The post office is five steps away. There I am posting my letters myself in order to play the role of the great feuilletonist of the *grande monde.* Of course, I am in close contact with Figaro, and to give you an idea of how harmless I can be, listen to the first of my two bad jokes:

Do not take the case Prado too hard. I am Prado, I am also father Prado, I dare say that I am also Lesseps . . . I wanted to give to my Parisians whom I love a new concept, that of a decent criminal. I am also Chambige—a gentleman criminal, too.

Second Joke. I send greetings to the immortals. M. Daudet belongs to the *quarante.*

Astu

What is inconvenient and hurts my modesty is that ultimately every name in history is I. With the children I put into the world matters likewise stand as follows. I have some misgivings as to whether or not all who get into "the Kingdom of God" also come *from* God. This fall I was present twice at my funeral, dressed as lightly as possible, first as Conte Robilant (—no, that is my son inasmuch as I am Carlo Alberto, my nature below), but Antonelli I was myself.

Dear Professor, you should see this monument. Since I am completely inexperienced in the things which I am creating you are entitled to any and all criticism. I am grateful but cannot give you the promise of putting it to good use: we artists are unteachable.

Today I went to see an operetta, genially Moorish. On that occasion I also made the pleasurable observation that now Moscow as well as Rome are grandiose. You see, even with respect to landscape you cannot deny me talent.

Just think, we will talk pleasantly pleasantly,—Turin is not far away, very serious duties in connection with our occupation are nonexistent at this time, a glass of Veltliner would have to be procured. Negligé in dress demanded by propriety.

Cordially and lovingly,

Your
Nietzsche

I walk everywhere in my student frock, here and there slap someone on the back and say: *Siamo contenti? son dio, ho fatto questa caricatura* . . .

Tomorrow my son Umberto is coming with the lovely Margherita whom I also receive only in shirt sleeves.

The *rest* for Frau Cosima . . . Ariadne . . . From time to time we practice witchcraft . . .

I had Caiaphas put in chains. I too was crucified last year by German physicians in a protracted fashion. Wilhelm Bismarck and all anti-Semites deposed.

You can make any use of this letter which will not lower me in the esteem of the people of Basel.—

www.ingramcontent.com/pod-product-compliance
Lightning Source LLC
Chambersburg PA
CBHW030511100426
42813CB00001B/3